People of the Wildcat Country

Tales from Badenoch and Strathspey

by

Sandra Macpherson

BIRLINN

First published in 2006 by
Birlinn Limited
West Newington House
10 Newington Road
Edinburgh
EH9 1QS

www.birlinn.co.uk

Copyright © Sandra Macpherson 2006

The moral right of Sandra Macpherson to be identified as the author
of this work has been asserted by her in accordance with the
Copyright, Designs and Patents Act 1988

ISBN10: 1 84158 448 7
ISBN13: 978 1 84158 448 5

British Library Cataloguing-in-Publication Data
A catalogue record for this book is available from the British Library

Typeset by Initial Typesetting Services, Edinburgh
Printed and bound by Creative Print and Design, Wales

For Catriona and Lachlan

Contents

	Foreword	vi
1	Glentruim	1
2	Macpherson Country	11
3	Past Times	23
4	A Small Hollow	33
5	The Raeburn Hut	41
6	The Spectre	51
7	The Airstrip	61
8	Loch Insh	73
9	Local Characters	81
10	The Hills	91
11	Uisge Beatha	105
12	Ruthven	115
13	The Souterrain	123
14	The Cairngorms	131
15	The Herd-Boy	143
16	Amongst the Heather	155
17	Highland Spirits	163
18	Hidden Loch	175
19	The Shelter	183
20	Games and Gatherings	193
	Epilogue: Between the Two Lights	203
	References	207

Foreword

My last book, *A Strange and Wild Place*, leaves the reader wondering what happened next in our lives, whether we managed to keep Glentruim or whether we lost the struggle that cost us so much heartache. In *People of the Wildcat Country* I relate the final parting from our home and how difficult it was to leave it behind. However, we took with us not only fond memories of Glentruim but also wonderful stories of those who lived around us in Badenoch and Strathspey.

I am grateful to Vicky Thain, Richard Seligman and Jo Clarke, who all took time to read my book, giving me comments and words of encouragement, and especially to Rosemary Perkins for her involvement and the many happy hours we spent together in connection with the manuscript.

Finally, many thanks to all those mentioned in the book who gave permission to write their stories. I am particularly grateful to Rob Ritchie, who kindly arranged meetings and also sourced information and old documents.

Badenoch and Strathspey indeed have much to offer, for not only is the landscape picuresque, but it is steeped in history. These are tales from some of the people who have lived in what I have called the Wildcat Country and loved it.

Sandra Macpherson
June 2006
Edinburgh

Between the Two Lights

Between the two lights the Gaelic people say,
A fisherman may cast a line into a shadowed pool and in the
Silver spray see an omened vision,
Of ancient ships and sailors hauling laden nets, their rhythmic
Songs and lusty shouts muted by a closing day.

Between the two lights the Gaelic people say,
A man may touch the skirt of heaven
And pass through death to life in spirit, and still return
In time to see departing day and greet the eve'n.

Between the two lights the Gaelic people say,
An amnesty gathers people who have fought throughout the days;
That witches and wizards sit spellbound, their potions
Grown cold, their barbs out of action
While Little Folk shake out the perfume
From bluebell, heather and bracken.

Between the two lights the Gaelic people say,
Eve, Adam and God walk gently through the garden
Speaking of heavenly truths, Divine promises and how to pray.
God sees their boredom, their touching hands,
Their pure delight
When suddenly He curtains day and beckons night.

(*Helen Macpherson, 1984*)

MAP OF THE CLAN COUNTRY

Kingcraig

Invereshie House

Loch Insh

A9

B970

Balavil

Ruthven Barracks

Kingussie

Pitmain

Ballachroan

A9

General Wade's Road

Nuide

A86

Newtonmore

Clan Macpherson House & Museum

Monadhliath Mountains

Creag Dhubh

Cluny's Cave

Glentruim

Ewan of the '45 Cairn

A9

River Truim

Lady Cluny Monument

River Spey

A86

Corrieyairack Pass

Cluny Castle

Gaskmore

Breakachy

Calum Piobair Cairn

A889

Cat Lodge

Laggan

Creag Ruadh

Dalchully

A86

Old Cluny's Monument

To Strathmashie
& St Kenneth's Church
Loch Laggan and
Ardverikie

To Halfway House

1

Glentruim

THE area of Badenoch and Strathspey is Macpherson country and I lived there for twenty-five years with my late husband, Euan, clan chieftain from, and our two children. Glentruim, the ancestral home of the Macphersons of Glentruim, is situated in the triangle of land bearing the same name between Dalwhinnie, Laggan and Newtonmore.

Reaching this historic clan land from the south means a journey up the A9, which now bypasses many small villages. In former times, passing trade was taken for granted, but now diversions and advertising contrive to entice tourists off the main road before they continue to their final destination.

It was new territory for me when I first arrived in winter all those years ago, yet I remember a feeling of home-coming as soon as we drove over the Drumochter Pass, down that famous stretch of road so often closed in bad weather, the gateway to the Highlands of Scotland. The hills on either side of this notorious road seemed to coax us into their wilderness, to catch us up in a vastness which closed behind us, as if to keep us from ever going back. When snow drifted, tarmac and ditches alike were obliterated. Stripes on the tops of long poles set in the ground on either side of the road acted as warnings, marking hidden depths, to remind us how treacherous the drifts could be. This could be a dangerous route in winter, which meant some Highland people were left stranded in solitude, obliged to deal with the bleak conditions in their own way. Eager to get to know the local people and learn the way of life in this picturesque part of Scotland, I looked forward to more clement days. Since time immemorial this had, after all, been the land not only of my husband's ancestors but also of the entire Clan Macpherson, whose motto is, 'Touch not the cat bot a glove.'

Badenoch lies in the valley of the Spey, about halfway between the North Sea and the Atlantic Ocean. This district, sometimes known as Upper Strathspey, stretches from Ben Alder to Rothiemurchus, flanked on either side by the Monadhliath Mountains, Glenfeshie Forest and the Forest of Mar. To the north-east is Craigellachie, and to the south-east rise the Grampian Mountains, which sweep from Loch Ericht and Ben Alder towards the Cairngorms. Loch Laggan lies to the south-west. It is a large strath which encompasses many tributaries of the River Spey, and is often flooded, particularly in winter, when the river bursts its banks while in spate. As one of the finest salmon rivers in Scotland (others being the Tay, the Dee and the Tweed), the Spey is important to the area.

In a guidebook compiled for the benefit of visitors to the district in 1930, it was noted that the construction of the Highland Railway made a great impact, giving easy access for tourists to enjoy Badenoch as a holiday resort. The book also states: 'An eminent London physician has compared the exhilarating effect of inhaling Badenoch air to that of imbibing the most sparkling champagne, with the very important difference that there is no risk of the loss of equilibrium or of an accompanying headache.' For those with certain ailments, the atmosphere was described as 'open-air treatment of chest diseases'.

Visitors in those days were considered so important to the area that they were all listed in each edition of the *Badenoch Herald*, along with a mention of the house in which they were staying. Such records show that the same people would come back year after year and the following generations seemed compelled to follow suit.

Romantic Badenoch, a guide book which delighted me, begins its narrative thus:

> In the land of the Macphersons,
> Where the Spey's wide waters flow;
> In the land where Royal Charlie
> Knew the best friend in his woe.

My first impression of Badenoch and Strathspey was that the countryside was suffused with a peaceful beauty, of a kind that seemed to calm the soul. The area had a great diversity of scenery, which constantly changed according to the time of year. Each season was as splendid as the others, each as exhilarating as the last. Had I had the time, I used to wish that I could have painted each scene, just as had Euan's Aunt Katie, from whom he inherited Glentruim.

I soon discovered that this place was full of traditions, beliefs and incredible tales. Coming from Edinburgh, it was like walking into an old book, full of pictures splashed with colour and descriptions of forgotten ways. The little villages were slow and sleepy in comparison with a modern capital. In many homes there was an absence of mod cons, which reflected the limited choice of household goods and provisions available in the local shops. The barter system, sensible and suitable for local purposes, was still in place for produce as well as services. There was an air of serenity, with no urgency, no rules other than good old-fashioned manners and etiquette. Everyone knew their place in society and appeared content with their accustomed way of life.

Like Glentruim, houses and crofts were passed on from one generation to the next, still occupied by descendents of the original family. The old families of the area told enchanting tales of their forebears and could look back on the hardships they had had to endure with nostalgia, not bitterness. I had a glimpse of this in my new life at Glentruim, our Macpherson family being steeped in history, where many traditions seemed to be of great importance. When I arrived, we were still piped into dinner on formal occasions and after the meal the ladies always left the men to their port and laughter, retiring to the drawing-room for coffee. Stone hot-water bottles aired the beds, and a scrubbing-board and mangle were used for the washing. Our housemaids, who wore black dresses with white frilly pinnies and mob-caps, all but curtseyed. In fact, I remember one making a 'bob' to visitors as she took their coats! At the age of twenty-two, I was embarrassed to have to ask staff to wear uniforms, but in those days no one objected up there. Some of the untrained girls were less than neat in these clothes and were clumsy when passing around drinks or food on trays, never really mastering the angle of the tray and thus allowing glasses to slide to the outer edge as they walked with a smile, oblivious of the spills.

We loved our home, which was a granite mansion built around 1826. It was large and rambling and in winter was probably just as uncomfortable to live in as some of the primitive croft- or black-houses! As it was cold and occasionally damp, I often resorted to hugging a hot-water bottle during the day as well as at night, and consequently had chilblains regularly. Little wonder the old housekeeper at Glentruim, Miss Sparrow, constantly wrung her hands! I too found myself doing this to take off the chill, then having to rub my numb fingers hard to get some feeling back. Pain in the fingers and toes, then a gradual tingling which trickled through as circulation improved, was a frequent occurrence. Miss Sparrow, incidentally, did not stay when I arrived, her loyalties to the lady of the house having died with my predecessor.

Privileged to live in the ancestral home, we worked tirelessly over the years to keep it for future generations. Our two children,

Catriona and Lachlan, both born in the early 1970s, grew up in a wonderful environment unique to the Highlands, where the beauty of the land, the peace, fresh air and way of life were special. We all benefited from living at Glentruim, and all worked hard, including the children. However, despite entertaining shooting guests, running a caravan park and renting out holiday cottages, besides undertaking other ventures over the years, the day finally arrived when we came to a halt.

By the late 1980s everything had come to crunch point. None of our arduous enterprises was going to make a financial impact on the upkeep of the estate. The love that we had for the place was gradually turning into a feeling of fear, the fear of loss. Euan and I sat in the drawing-room, surrounded by family portraits, and they all looked down scornfully as we discussed the future of Glentruim.

By this time, Euan had retired. He was twenty years my senior, but the age gap was never obvious, for he was always very good-looking, with abundant energy and unbelievable strength, even into his later years. He would tackle any task on the estate and could labour harder and longer than those he worked with. What is more, he never stopped until a job was done, sometimes working long after the estate-workers had gone home.

The 'doom and gloom' conversation had raised its ugly head so many times over the years. It forced us to launch into new businesses, eternally confident that our next idea would bring success. This pattern always caused me to tremble inside. Euan would be so low in spirits that it would be difficult for him to see a future at Glentruim. I would drive myself impossibly hard to make a success of the various ventures I had to juggle to complement the income from shooting and fishing parties, the holiday cottages and the caravan park. All this and bringing up two children! Luckily I enjoyed a challenge, and a challenge was certainly what I was given in the north.

We thought of turning Glentruim into a nursing home, for after all, I was a state-registered nurse and Euan, a psychologist, had been very eminent in Scotland. He had inherited Glentruim just after I qualified in Edinburgh, so I had not in fact practised nursing since the 1960s, but we did not view that as a problem. We looked into this prospect and although the house was big enough and conversions were possible, the drainage and water supply were inadequate for the purpose. This idea for Glentruim had to be abandoned, but we started to look at nursing homes for sale.

Our search resulted in the purchase of a suitable establishment in Stirlingshire. It was a good business and after the first year of trading we bought a flat close by. The idea was to run the nursing home during the week and go back to Glentruim at the weekends. The mansion had become our 'holiday cottage'. However, we continued to entertain at Glentruim from time to time, particularly during the Clan Gathering, held each year on the first weekend in August. Every year since our arrival at Glentruim we had hosted a large tea-party for members of the Clan Macpherson. This was always held on the lawns in front of Glentruim on the Sunday after church and the habit was never broken until we sold up.

We had just one more large, unforgettable celebration at Glentruim; our daughter's wedding. There were to be two venues after the marriage ceremony at Laggan church, the first being for champagne and smoked salmon on the lawns of Glentruim, where photographs were to be taken, and the second a reception, dinner and dance at the Duke of Gordon Hotel in Kingussie.

I thought that everything had been planned to perfection, but one element you could never depend on at Glentruim was the water supply. The men were busy erecting the marquee on the top lawns, our gun team of four was busy preparing the two cannons on the lower lawns for the celebratory firings later in the day and the ladies were on the way to the hairdresser in Kingussie. What could be worse on a wedding day, with the house bursting at the seams with people, than no water? We had guests in every room, even in the two small rooms up the tower, about twenty of us in all. Two men went off with the Range Rover and trailer carrying an enormous drum, which was to be filled with water from Newtonmore. This water was for the men, whereas we ladies went to the Duke of Gordon for baths, then came home and changed.

Charlie Millar from the Duke of Gordon had everything in hand, including the impressive classic cars which were to take the wedding party to and from the church. Refreshed and changed, we arrived at the church to find it already packed with over 200 guests. I remember thinking that there were too many cars for the little narrow roads of Laggan and wondered how many were in fact taking advantage of the bus. The bus too was full, I later noticed. We had thought that most guests would go straight to the hotel and only a few would return to Glentruim for the photographs. Our thoughts proved wrong, but it was wonderful to see everyone on our own lawns. However, it was the chain of events that Charlie told me about later that was particularly amusing.

It was a beautiful summer's day and the view across the valley from Glentruim was, as always, stunning, stretching far down the valley towards the Cairngorms, with the rocks of Creag Dubh on one side and gentle wilderness on the other. Bruce Macpherson played his pipes for the happy couple as champagne and smoked salmon were handed out to the guests. Those attending were blissfully unaware of the goings-on behind the scenes. Charlie had begun to worry about the champagne supply when he saw the number of cars arriving in a long, slow procession up the avenue, and sent for more from the hotel. By this time the person in charge of the cars was diverting them to the farm drive.

In the meantime the gunners were filling the cannons with gunpowder and wadding ready to fire. The bride and groom and also the bridesmaids each had a turn at firing, which resulted in intriguing pictures for the wedding album. Paulo Satney, a well-known photographer originally from Prague and now based in Aviemore, took remarkable shots, some of which he displayed in his shop window for quite some time after the event. The gunners were the only ones wearing ear-muffs, so the photographs show beautiful girls with screwed-up faces and fingers in their ears, surrounded by clouds of smoke. There are other photographs of people in fits of laughter as their friends disappear in different shades of smoke containing the odd burnt shred of rag from the blast.

My mother was in one of the first cars to go off to the hotel and apparently the driver had difficulty in getting back up our drive when he returned. Cars were parked bumper to bumper, 'and they were still coming', Charlie laughed as he told me, 'car after car after car!' It was the bus that concerned him most, for with cars parked all up one side, there was not enough room for a bus. He had warned the bus driver that there was a sheer drop halfway up, on the north side, and that on no account should he drive on the verge. Charlie frantically tried to find one of his other staff members to assist, but just as he spotted him, his employee too was engulfed in smoke from the cannons and obliterated from sight.

Once we all finally got to 'The Duke' there was a sigh of relief from Charlie and the rest of the evening went as planned. It was important and seemed right to us that we were at Glentruim for our daughter's wedding, and we were fortunate still to be living there. Like all celebrations at Glentruim, it will be remembered. Here was a bond between two people that would be noted forever on the vast Macpherson tree.

Apart from myself, Glentruim was first in Euan's heart. His yacht *Legacy*, which we acquired during the early years of running the nursing home, was a very close second. We kept *Legacy* at Dunstaffanage, near Oban, on the west coast. As time went by, we spent more and more weekends sailing and fewer at Glentruim. When we sold much of the estate, the sea became a comfort to Euan, for he felt at peace and could put the thought of forsaking Glentruim out of his mind.

Although Glentruim was being looked after by caretakers, it had become increasingly damp and sad-looking without the family. We did not enjoy opening it up for only fleeting visits and Clan Gatherings, and felt guilty that we could not be there all of the time. Evidence of neglect was creeping in, and so it seemed appropriate to sell the house, the farms, the various cottages and most of the land. We were keen to see Glentruim permanently maintained and lived in again; absentee landlords were not good for the area. We could possibly have gone back, but by then our way of life and our attitudes had changed.

It took weeks to pack box after box, from cellars to towers, from cottages to garages and sheds. This must have been the most difficult thing I have ever done in my life and it affected Euan desperately. He was never really the same again. The past haunted him; he missed Glentruim, as did I. Living in the central belt of Scotland never seemed right with Glentruim gone, so about ten years later we decided to sell the nursing home too. Our next plan was to buy a house in Edinburgh as a base and then charter boats all over the world. Having achieved my skipper's certificate and sailed with Euan on the west coast and around the islands, I was very enthusiastic about the idea. Euan was a superb yachtsman and I felt quite confident that what we were about to do was right. As soon as the nursing home was sold we started looking for property in Edinburgh. In the meantime, we had booked our first charter, three weeks in the West Indies. Life began to look exciting, but not for long.

Euan had a stroke in 1998, the week before we were due to go on our first sailing holiday. Our world fell apart overnight and was never to be the same again. The houses I had looked at in Edinburgh would not have suited our needs, particularly after Euan's second stroke, which took place on the way to look at yet another, more suitable, house. The next stroke was the worst and happened the morning after we moved into our new home. But even then, we tried to make life as normal as possible, going to the theatre, eating out and having dinner parties. He was very brave and truly struggled with aspects of daily living. He died when we were out for dinner one night with close friends. This was the week before our thirty-fourth wedding anniversary, and on that date, 14 June 2002, a friend handed me a gold charm which Euan had arranged to have made, with her assistance. He always gave me a charm for my bracelet on our anniversary and this particular year it was very apt: it was our initials entwined together; entwined as our lives had been through happy days at Glentruim and more troubled ones too.

Roddy Martine wrote in Euan's obituary:

'He will be remembered by those who knew him for his profound intelligence, and latterly for the courage which enabled him to retain his dignity while fully aware of his physical limitations.

'Others will remember him as a gentleman of the old school, beautifully mannered and courteous, a Renaissance man in a modern world: a wit, raconteur and a generous companion.

'Clan Macpherson has lost a distinguished chieftain. The loss to his friends and family is immeasurable.'

In writing my first book, *A Strange and Wild Place*, which was cathartic for me, I told of our life in our ancestral home and stories connected with Glentruim. There are certainly more, as well as tales of other places and people in Badenoch and Strathspey, which are worthy of mention in the following chapters.

2

Macpherson Country

TO be a Macpherson, living in Macpherson country and able to bring up a family in the ancestral home, was a privilege. We had Glentruim for nearly twenty-five years, where, above the junction of the Spey and the Truim, Invernahavon was tucked away. Pronounced 'Inver-na-han', this was a famous battlefield where the Macphersons and Campbells fought the Redcoats. Invernahavon means 'the parting of the waters' and it was overlooking this historical place that Mary Macpherson, the daughter of a parish schoolmaster, lived in a croft. She was renowned for her poems and although she was lame and of portly bearing, it was said that she was a striking figure as she ventured out in her blue cloak and a white mutch (headgear), as was her custom.

In that valley, which was full of folklore and superstition, it used to be believed that there was a spring at Invernahavon which cured toothache. I remember taking the children down to the bottom fields there with coat-hangers as water diviners, in search of this well. There were also superstitions surrounding other places in the valley. For instance, there was reputed to be a well behind Torcroy at Glentromie that cured warts; and it was said that the folk at Loch Laggan would occasionally see fairies milking the deer. I have also heard that there is a stone on the hill road between Laggan and Dalwhinnie where food and gifts were left for the fairies.

Superstitions were taken quite seriously in the Highlands in the old days, and as Badenoch and Strathspey was Macpherson country, there were bound to be tales connected to Macphersons. One particular Macpherson worthy of a mention has been written about by many, but not all have the same story. This was Captain John Macpherson. Everyone in Badenoch and Strathspey knows one version or another regarding his life and the catastrophe at Gaick. These narratives can be found as far back as 1800 in the *Scots Magazine* and even Sir Walter Scott wrote about him in the *Foreign Quarterly* during the year of 1827. In 1900, in *The Clan Chattan Papers*, Alexander Macpherson wrote about 'these distorted and imaginative versions, all apparently derived from superstitious native sources'.

Captain Macpherson of the 82nd regiment was born at Glentruim in 1724 and was the second son of Alexander Macpherson of Phones, which was a short distance from Glentruim. Their chieftains were the Macphersons of Invereshie. This Macpherson, Iain Dubh MacAlastair as he was known in those days in Badenoch, was described as the Black Officer (Othaichear Dubh), for his black heart, some say, while others say it was more for his looks. He was disliked and feared by many. It was also thought that evil was within him and that he dealt with the devil. He was twenty years the senior of his wife, the same age gap as in my marriage, which was often the case in the Highlands. Captain Macpherson's main military duty was recruiting, which he carried out with great enthusiasm, and he regularly tricked local lads into enlisting with King George's Army. He trapped all those he could and it was even said that he forcibly enlisted 'well-proportioned parsons, who might possibly fight better than they preached'.

Many Highlanders, including the folk in Badenoch, enjoyed a dram or two, and the Black Officer would take advantage of this. He would invite young men into the inns and when they were well inebriated, he would slip a king's shilling into their pockets. Then he would tell them that they had to join the king's army.

When they asked why, he would say that they had accepted the king's shilling and, if they doubted this, to feel in their pockets! On finding the shilling piece they knew that they were duty-bound to enlist. Mothers were forever lamenting these cherished sons, who, although in some cases useless, were made to don the 'red coat' unwillingly while the Black Officer 'reaped more than the usual measure of opprobrium'. Those young men that were tricked in such a manner would be kept in dungeons beneath Ballachroan, the home of the Black Officer. When he had gathered enough recruits he would send them out under escort.

Another ploy of the Black Officer was to dress up as his shepherd and entice travellers into a bothy. There would be no food there for the visitors, but he used to say that he would happily kill a sheep for them, which he did. They were to keep this secret and not tell his 'master', he would tell them. Captain Macpherson would then go home and come back later with his shepherd, both wearing their own clothes this time. Hence the travellers would be caught red-handed eating a sheep that did not belong to them, which they had unwittingly received by deception. The gallows was the penalty for sheep rustling, but they were told that they would be spared this fate if they promised to enlist. Hanging was certainly used as the penalty for stealing sheep in the area and there was even an old tree at Glentruim, up a rough pathway called Pelhams Drive, where thieves were hanged for sheep rustling. This track through the woods was a favourite walk of mine in my time at Glentruim. On dry, warm summer days you could hear small twigs snap beneath your feet and the aroma of birch would fill the air, an overwhelming smell that would almost make you feel dizzy in the heat. On either side of this narrow, unkempt grassy path were tall trees, whose overhanging branches would occasionally open slightly in the wind to allow the hot sun to filter through.

Although there are not many stories of the Black Officer's military adventures, there was, however, a tale passed on from a boatman at Loch Awe describing an incident when the Black Officer was engaged with a British force in India fighting the French. It was said that he alone survived in this battle and carried on shooting the French over a wall of corpses. He had volunteered to make a tunnel to enable his soldiers to get into a neighbouring town, but the French, realising this, blew up the tunnel and, according to the boatman, the Black Officer's body was found 'all black with smoke'. However, as the story goes, he was brought to life again by some supernatural power.

When the Black Officer retired from the Army, he reinstated the family farm at Ballachroan. He took old stones from an abandoned parish church in Kingussie to build his new steading wall, but this action was very much frowned upon by the villagers, for they regarded it as the work of the Devil. They never lost an opportunity to see the work of Satan in his progress, whether personal or business.

The year before a notable catastrophe, the Black Officer had attempted to get together a shooting party, but only one person arrived at their prearranged meeting place. It was Post Bane who turned up and he tried to dissuade the captain from setting off, but Macpherson replied that this was impossible since he had an appointment in Gaick that he was obliged to attend. The two men and their dogs set off together for the bothy there and, when they arrived, settled in for the night in front of the fire. The Black Officer seemed agitated, according to his companion, who also noticed that he had had a fair amount to drink. Just before midnight the dogs growled fiercely, pulling on their leashes, and the captain began to tremble. There was a knock on the door, which he answered, telling his friend to remain where he was, wrapped in his blanket for the night. The door was only opened a crack before the captain quickly went out to speak to his visitor, shutting the door firmly behind him.

Post Bane heard him say that he would be back with more men the following year, at the same time. He was pale and visibly shaken when he came back in and after calming himself with a dram, said that the person at the door was a friend who was to join the shooting party but had changed his mind since so few had turned up. Post Bane, thinking it was a long distance to come only to turn back, was told by the captain that this was no problem since the visitor had a swift horse. The next morning Post Bane looked for prints in the track outside, discovering to his horror only the mark of a cloven hoof. This was yet more proof that the Black Officer was in league with the Devil.

The aforementioned catastrophe took place during the first week of January, which was when Christmas was celebrated in former times. On Christmas Eve in 1800 the captain, then approaching his seventy-fifth year, again organised a shooting party and planned to take his huntsman to the bothy at Gaick. Of the circumstances surrounding the disaster, Alexander Macpherson wrote in 1990 that the accounts had 'been made the constant theme and vehicle of the wildest and most improbable fictions – from the silly and superstitious tales of the common country people down to the bombastic fustian of the full-blown romance of Mr James Grant'. One does wonder, with few forms of entertainment in those days other than their own, how easy it would have been for tales to be exaggerated whilst being passed on from one person to the next.

Word of the winter shoot soon got around the valley and when invitations were imminent, men made themselves scarce so as not to have to accept the offer. No one wanted to cross the Black Officer, and no one wished to go into the black and wild glen where there had been stories of witches and demons, reinforced by the events of the previous Christmas Eve. However, a party of five went, the Black Officer and four friends. Others followed in a second party, but they turned back when the shoes of Post Bane's son fell apart, leaving him barefoot: thoughts of supernatural intervention had got the better of them. The Black Officer and his friends never returned. The bothy was destroyed in an avalanche and it took six hours to dig out the bodies from the rubble, which had been covered by deep snow drifts. It was recorded that the guns were found broken and twisted and the dogs died with 'looks of terror about them'.

A local resident at the time described the hills surrounding the Forest of Gaick as being steep, smooth and bare, which made the glen subject to avalanches in severe stormy weather. A gentleman of the valley, whilst out stalking a herd of ten deer, also reported that he had seen 'a rolling volume of snow descend the mountain', which 'buried them in its bosom'. An avalanche might have been a more realistic explanation for the Gaick catastrophe if common-sense had prevailed instead of the superstition which had been so insidiously instilled through myths of witchcraft and the Devil. Mrs Grant from the Manse of Laggan, who lived not far from Ballachroan and was a close friend of the Black Officer, described the incident as being the effects of a whirlwind or avalanche which destroyed the hut, burying the men in the ruins.

In my view, either of the above two explanations is possible. Avalanches have certainly been recorded in the Highlands and in the early 1980s, as a family, we watched the vortex of a tornado travel across the sky from Laggan to Glentruim before scooping up the shower blocks in the caravan site and depositing them several yards down the field. They landed upside down: pedestals and basins were scattered in the grass. This whirlwind also blew through our conservatory, taking with it two sides of the structure. Shattered glass was sprinkled all over the avenue and up the top bank behind the house.

The Black Officer was seventy-six when he died and was buried at St Columba's churchyard, Kingussie. The stories about him became legendary and some fables recounted ghostly happenings in the Forest of Gaick. They told of frightening voices, shouting, laughter and the singing of immoral songs. Then there were screams, pleas for mercy and the sound of dogs howling. Nothing was ever actually seen: it was only the ghostly voices and noises that were heard by the terrified people they tormented and so it was not known whose spirits had been out there. It was presumed that they were the Black Officer and his friends who perished that fatal Christmas Eve.

Not all in the valley believed what was said of the Black Officer, nor the superstitions that surrounded his memory. 'Old Biallid', Captain Lachlan Macpherson, who was one of the Black Officer's closest friends, held him in high regard. His friends found him to be a kind and generous clansman who would liberally assist others, even to the detriment of his own affairs, but it seems that the Black Officer was constantly engaged in litigation and he in fact died bankrupt. However, according to Old Biallid, he was 'active, intelligent, and superior in all things, a dangerous enemy, but an unshaken ally; and the most bitter foe had only to seek his amity and he immediately became his friend'. Perhaps we should heed the words of those who knew the Black Officer well, rather than believe the opinions of local kinsmen who were misled through superstition and the occult. After the Black Officer lost his wife, he spent most of his days alone on the hills of Gaick with only his dogs by his side. 'Such was one of the last true deer-stalkers of the old race of gentlemen – a man who, if we lived 100 years, we should not see his like again', was how Old Biallid spoke of him.

Being married into the Macpherson family, naturally I find the Macpherson history fascinating. I cannot miss out one other Macpherson, James, known as the Gipsy Outlaw, who was a magnificent musician and played the fiddle. Strathspey has always been known to be synonymous with the music of the fiddle. The area is filled with music and the Strathspey is the name given to a tune for a dance of slower tempo which precedes the 'spirited graceful foursome reel'. The fiddle has been described as the 'unpretentious Scots word for the violin, particularly played for dancing', but it and the bagpipes were not the only important instruments in the Highlands. In earlier years the clarsach, the ancient Scottish harp, which I have enjoyed playing since the early 1970s, 'was the instrument for the diversion of the upper part of local society'. Indeed, there are records of lairds of Badenoch having their own clarsach players as early as the mid-seventeenth century. Many a tale crossed the valley through music; this was often the way that news travelled, bad or good. Instruments such as the clarsach and fiddle were played at ceilidhs, merry gatherings where there was spontaneous entertainment. The Free Church (a strict, Calvinistic branch of the Presbyterian Church) frowned upon ceilidhs and banned music and dancing, considering these casual musical occasions as 'wiles of the "Evil One"'! It would be the menfolk, with only a few of the women, who would gather together during the long winter evenings for a ceilidh. The event would be hosted by the Fear an Tigh, 'the man of the house', who would probably commence with a poem or piece of music, which would encourage others to contribute to the amusement of the evening. The last authentic ceilidh house, purported to be in Lewis, was burnt down according to the owner's instructions as he sailed away in an emigrant ship. Ceilidhs still take place but unfortunately not in quite the same way. They now seem to be as organised as a theatre performance: there are no surprises for today's audience when artistes are listed in a programme.

An old ledger containing longhand notes tells of James Macpherson, the Gipsy Outlaw, who was hanged in Banff in 1700. A talented fiddler, he attended many dances and ceilidhs with his instrument, which made him very unpopular with the church back in those days. He is recorded as having been a good-looking, tall man, who was around twenty-four at the time of his execution.

The writings tell us that a Macpherson of Invereshie, while intoxicated at a grand wedding in the north of Scotland, was attracted to a beautiful gipsy girl. Their relationship resulted in a baby boy, James, who was brought up by his father. Macpherson of Invereshie was killed while chasing after members of another clan who had stolen his cattle. From then on young James Macpherson was brought up by his gipsy family. Yet the clansmen 'clothed and fed mother and son and made sure that they always had money. As we say in the old way he grew up to beauty, strength and stature rarely equalled.' James was also known to be skilled in the use of different swords, including the claymore.

It is also mentioned that 'for reasons unknown he became a "freebooter" and the captain of a band of gipsies'. In records of those times, gipsies were known as Egyptians! With his compatriots, he broke into houses and stole cattle and horses, but he was never known to commit crimes of 'personal cruelty', as it was described, or 'to touch the helpless and distressed' , nor 'was any murder carried out by his command'.

James was tricked by a young girl who had been bribed by the magistrates in Aberdeen, and he was captured. However, one market day his cousin Donald Macpherson assisted his escape, along with others, including a James Gordon. Following this they were captured at Keith whilst attending a summer's eve fair. James and his associates were taken to Banff and put into prison. He was brought to trial on 7 November 1700. The sentence was pronounced as follows:

> For sai muckle as you James Macpherson and James Gordon pannals, are found guilty by ane verdict of ane assyse to be knowne holden and repute to be Egyptians and vagabonds and oppressors of his Maties, free lieges in ane bangstree manner and going up and donne the country armed and keeping the mercats in ane hostile manner and that you are thieves and receptors of thieves and that you are pessima forma. Therefore, the Sherrif Depute of Banff and I in his name a judge and decernes, yon the s'd James

Macpherson and James Gordon to be taken to the cross of
Banff from the tollbooth thereof where you now lye and
there upon ane gibbet to be erected to be hanged by the
neck to the death by the hand of the common executioner
upon Friday next week being the 16 November instant,
being a public weekly mercat day betwixt the hours of
between two and three in the afternoon and in the
meantime declares their haile novele goods and gear to be
in brought to the fiscall for his Maties interest and so
recommends this sentence to be seen put in execution by
the Magistrates of Banff.

What this amounted to was that James Macpherson had been
accused of 'going up and down the country armed, and keeping
the markets in a hostile manner'. This was not much proof of
crimes punishable by hanging. After James was sentenced the
Sheriff asked if he had any requests and, not surprisingly, he
requested his fiddle. Every night before his hanging he played
laments on his instrument and crowds gathered outside his cell
to hear him play. Each night more people came to listen, some
becoming more and more distressed as his time drew near.

On the day that James was to be hanged, he knew that a
pardon was coming from Badenoch, so he began to play his
fiddle to fill in time. But the authorities were corrupt and put the
clock forward twenty minutes so that James would be hanged
before the pardon arrived. James realised that his fate was near
and offered his fiddle to anyone in the waiting crowd of spectators. Being superstitious, none of them took him up on his
offer. James raised the fiddle and broke it across his knee, threw
it into the crowd, then jumped from the ladder and was hanged.
He was no sooner dead than a man on horseback was seen to be
approaching with a written pardon in his hand.

Gallow Hill, where James was executed, became a notable
place of death, since he was the last person to receive capital

punishment in Scotland under heritable jurisdiction. In time, his fate may be forgotten by some, but his compositions will be recognised and played forever by lovers of traditional music.

'The Macpherson's Rant', which was composed by James and was often sung by the young woman who loved him, is also known as 'The Macpherson's Farewell'. The 'Farewell Rant', 's fheudar dhomh fhinn a bhi falbh dhach aidh direach,' (I must myself be going home directly), is part of our folk-music tradition today and is used for the Macpherson March every year when the Macpherson Clan is piped across the Spey Bridge to the Newtonmore Games in August. Robert Burns, too, commended James and dedicated the following verse to this great musician:

> Sae rantingly, sae wantonly,
> Sae dauntingly gaid he;
> He played a tune and danced it aroon'
> Alow the gallows tree.

James' fiddle and bow were retrieved and eventually taken to the Macpherson Clan Museum in Newtonmore. The Banff clock, which was in pieces, was also brought to the museum.

Another musical treasure kept in the Clan Museum is a black chanter, Feadan Dhubh. According to tradition, this chanter fell miraculously from Heaven to rally the Macphersons at the 'notoriously savage clan fight' which took place in Perth in 1396. The Macphersons are proud of their museum, which has a fine collection of portraits, keepsakes and volumes of historical documents, all of great interest to the many visitors that pass through the doors each year.

3

Past Times

BEFORE we arrived at Glentruim, when Euan's uncle, Duncan, was the laird, there was a dairy farm on the estate. Billy Cowan was brought up there and told me that as a child he always enjoyed listening to all the stories his father related about his strong-willed employer. 'My father and the laird never got on,' Billy recalled. 'I remember when they fell out for four months! They would be out cutting wood for stacks and the laird would come along and create. He would always have his gun on his shoulder and his springer at his heels. His dog was always at his side as he followed my father around, niggling, niggling.'

The Cowans left Glentruim for a while but returned after the war. It was amusing to hear how Billy's father was enticed back to Glentruim. Urgent repairs were required on some farm machinery, so Uncle Duncan, having fallen out with his new farm manager, was obliged to turn to Cowan, who was the best mechanic he knew for the purpose. Numerous notes were sent backwards and forwards between the laird and Billy's father, with the laird asking advice and eventually, as he had intended all along, requesting his return. Billy's father accepted.

Those were carefree days at Glentruim, when life was gentle. Once, as young Billy was cycling up the avenue to the Big House with a basket full of butter fresh from the Home Farm, his handle-bars suddenly locked, he went over the top and all the butter landed in pine needles. So it was back to the farm to pick out the needles, reshape the butter and return to deliver it, as if nothing had happened.

The Laird of Glentruim and Billy's father seemed to have some sort of understanding and accepted their mutual intolerance. Had they not, the next incident I heard about could easily have led to dismissal. Billy's father had been out with a scythe, opening up a path for new drains, with two or three slices of backs (pieces of wood) ready for use, when the laird came up the drive and asked his chauffeur to stop the car. Yet again there was a falling out, which took place at the entrance to Glentruim. 'The laird stepped out and they had a ding-dong,' as Billy put it, with a smile on his face. 'What's that there, stretching up into the heavens?' asked the laird. 'You know damn fine what that is,' was the farm manager's reply, 'and if you had paid for gates you wouldn't be saying that.' Glentruim had obviously decided to have his workers make new gates at the entrance rather than buy them! The laird strode back to his car, slapped his knee with his hand and in a rage asked McRae, his chauffeur, 'Have you ever been at a pantomime, McRae?'

Cowan even got into trouble when he was doing the laird a favour. Frequently he would be asked to drive up to Dalwhinnie to collect crates of whisky for the laird and on one of these occasions he was reprimanded for hurtling too fast up the drive. Having been asked if he had just come up the avenue and admitting that he had, he was told that he had driven 'like a bloody sky-rocket'. 'Yes, with a crate of your whisky', was his reply.

The hereditary clan chiefs and their chieftains have often been strong, somewhat eccentric characters, occasionally even autocratic, and Euan was no exception. He took after his uncle in many ways, in all but appearance. In full Highland dress he certainly typified his breed, every inch the spruce, handsome laird, so much so that photographs of him are featured in many of the tourist books promoting Scotland even today.

In previous centuries, when a Highland clan was said to be based on 'war and the family', battles were common. The clans fought for the sake of honour and prestige, or merely for better grazing, cattle and sheep. Although the chief and his clan all wore the same tartan, intermingled socially and shared the same kind of life, he was indisputably in charge, making his own rules and administering justice within his domain. The clan itself has always been an extended family, with all members, no matter how distantly related, considered 'cousins'; the ideal of the close-knit family still continues, whereas clan battles have long since ceased!

There may have been fierce battles between the clans, but nevertheless there were also days of ceilidhs in the crofts and cottages, where the pibroch, song, dancing and poetry were all prevalent. 'Girls knitted, boys busked their fishing hooks, and peeled willow-wands for baskets. The harvesters sang in time to the strokes of the sickle; the boat-men sang at their oars in the chief's galley; the women sang while waulking [kneading] the cloth, one singing the verse, the others joining in the chorus; the islemen sang as they gathered the seaweed.' This was the way in which the news and stories found their way from one end of the valley to the next.

Crofts are agricultural holdings, many of which used to be occupied by clansmen of their respective chiefs. In early times the chief of a clan would expect military service in lieu of rent, but years later rents were paid in cash, in a system ultimately governed by several Crofting Acts. Donnie and Elizabeth Wilson still live on a farm not very far from Glentruim and Donnie told me about his childhood at Drummin, situated at the foot of the Corrieyarrick. His parents arrived there after the First World War, when his father took up the post of under-stalker to Sir John

Ramsden of Ardverikie. The factor, a hard man, only allowed them to keep as many animals as could be wintered on the place, but since there were no fences, restricting the livestock cannot have been easy. Life in those days was indeed demanding, for Donnie's father would cut hay early in the morning before leaving for his work, and would expect Donnie and his sister to have it spread before he returned.

During the 1940s there were about thirty families in crofts around Crathie, sadly now all gone. Older members died and the younger ones moved away when changes such as the building of the dam at Loch Laggan, with the subsequent loss of croft land, forced them to travel further afield to find employment. Interestingly, Donnie assisted the very last resident in Crathie with his flitting (moving out) from a croft cottage that was later deliberately burned down because it posed a danger. However derelict, it should instead have been saved as a reminder of what life was like not so very long ago, and preserved for posterity. It is sad that so many of the old dwellings in the region have been similarly lost. As Donnie quite rightly stated, 'Today we are threatened by the "march of the bungalows", which are sometimes grossly bigger.'

Families spent many a day out in the fields cutting peat, which was used as fuel for open fires in their dwellings. The turfs would be cut, neatly placed in rows, dried and gathered in for the winter. Certain conditions in peat bogs allow the plant life that grows in the stagnant water not to decay, but rather to remain and accumulate, giving preservative properties to the peat that eventually forms. In 1927 the local newspaper recorded that two peat-cutters had discovered a skeleton buried under two feet of moss on Dava Moor, six miles north of Grantown. The bottom half of the skeleton was wrapped in a strongly woven cloth and on the shoulders was a shepherd's tartan plaid. It was extra-ordinary to read that a Balmoral cap that had been placed on the middle of the body was so well-preserved that every strand of its corded material was intact. Above the cap was 'a cudgel four feet long'. Following investigation, it was concluded that the skeleton was that of a woman, whose clothes were dated back 150 years from the date of the find! Such is proof of the capacity of peat to preserve.

Fir roots too were collected from formerly forested land and heaped into a pile, along with fir cones, which gave out an even incandescence in the versatile open fires that served for both heating and cooking. Before the cruisie (an old-fashioned, open lamp) and later paraffin lamps, strips of resinous torch fir were used as candles. These fir candles, stored for the winter, were often the only source of light during a long winter's evening. They would always be kept with the kindling beside the peat fire, to be lit and then pushed into a special place in the wall, where they burned surprisingly brightly. It was the responsibility of the man of the house to light the first sliver, afterwards uttering a prayer, a ritual to expel any fears in the blackness of the night.

The simple houses glowed with warmth, gently lit by Aladdin's lamps that not only produced extra heat but also formed dancing images on walls, suggesting secret and mystical messages. There would not have been enough light for much reading, but there would have been knitting, storytelling and singing. Black pots hung from hooks on chains or sat on shelves at each side of the fire. In them porridge, soup and stews would simmer for hours, perhaps all night. For baking, there was a particular pot with a concave lid, into the hollow of which peat cinders were placed to encourage cakes to rise. Even the 'box' iron would be heated from the fire, by means of a flap at the back which was lifted so that a red-hot brick could be inserted. There was no such thing as an ironing-board; the ironing was done on the kitchen table, usually covered with a cloth or blanket.

In those days no local authority took responsibility for keeping roads open during the long, hard winters. Therefore, in the certain knowledge of impending isolation, the crofters had to make their own contingency plans. In the late autumn, provisions were carefully stored, including a boll (140 lb) of flour, oatmeal and sugar, and about 14 lb of potatoes. The latter were pitted, meaning that a long trench had to be dug, with the soil piled up on either side, after which the potatoes would be dropped in and then covered with dry bracken before the soil was shovelled back over the top.

Everyone grew his own oats, turnips and potatoes in the garden, unlike today when better transport has facilitated the purchase of fresh vegetables in the district. In the early eighteenth century, before the introduction of potatoes and turnips, the traditional staple diet would have been brose made from oatmeal, varieties of mealy pudding and, of course, porridge. Whipped cream and oatmeal, a dish known as Athol brose, is still offered as a Scottish dessert today. In former times charms would sometimes have been hidden in puddings such as these, with oatmeal sprinkled on the top.

At Glentruim we had much in common, even in the early 1970s, with those who lived there before us. Donnie told me that in his father's time there was no butcher's meat, only game – hare, rabbit and plenty of venison – which was largely the same for us in our early days at Glentruim, when we made full use of game from the estate. However, Donnie's father's family was fortunate enough to receive a rigg lamb during the times of clipping; this was given to him in return for faithful service. In preparation for winter, these meats would be put into a barrel of salt, which acted as a preservative in the absence of a deep-freeze.

During the long winters sleighs drawn by ponies would have been the only form of transport. At other times the ponies would work a 'gig' or 'ralli-car'. I, too, relied on ponies many a time, particularly for ferrying the children to and from the school car, which stopped three miles away down the Glentruim back road. This was a wonderful way to start the day, with my younger child in front of me as I rode bare-back and the older one behind on her own pony with a lunging rein between us. Ponies are still used in the Highlands for carrying deer carcases down from the hill. In previous times they often had panniers each side of the saddle when taken out for the day during the shooting season.

The crofters made all their own hay and cut it with a scythe. Only later would machinery be brought in, initially crude mowers with three-foot cutter bars, each of which had a knife-edge on the inside. One of these was given to Donnie's family by a shooting tenant and was used for many years. What a complete contrast of lives there was between the crofters and the wealthy tenants! It must have been very difficult for them to fully comprehend each other's ways.

I knew myself how difficult it was to manage unaided in isolation, having had to look after Glentruim alone for over a year while Euan finished his job in Edinburgh. Some of the work was heavy: sacks of coal had to be stacked into the Land Rover and delivered to our holiday cottages, and rubbish from all the houses on the estate had to be taken to the A9 for collection.

Like many others, Donnie's family relied on travellers and tramps passing by to assist during the summer months. These people would be offered accommodation in a basic bothy containing a comfortable bed in exchange for labour. They would also receive bread and hot soup in the evening and porridge for breakfast. It was not uncommon to see the same people come by each year; indeed, they were expected and sadly missed if they did not return. The visitors would be a mixed bunch, from habitual travellers to intelligent businessmen who had 'dropped out' of society. 'Money had nothing to do with it; these were not all paupers, they chose this way of life,' Donnie told me. 'One person in particular, who claimed to be a carpenter, stopped his journey short to lend a hand.' It was a story Donnie remembered well. His father went off to some sheepdog trials, leaving their visitor to work on a new body for their wheelbarrow. This new 'hand' took advantage of the terms, for on his return, Donnie's father saw no wheelbarrow, only a very large bag of kindling! The barrow had been too much of a challenge!

Then there were the tinkers who regularly came through the valley, although today they would be called 'travellers' rather than tinkers. But what shame is there in being a tinker? They were professional tinsmiths, who took their name through making goods in tin, mainly mugs, remoulding new or old pieces of the material from food containers into some kind of useful utensil. When they arrived at the door there would be a short period of bargaining for their tin wares, which included pails, skillets, milk basins, jugs and mugs. Occasionally they also had for sale clothes-pegs tied with tin, pot scrubbers and even besoms, which were floor brushes made out of heather. It was said that Glentruim heather was the best for making brooms and pot scrubbers. Tin mugs were the tinkers' best-seller and would often be attached to the belts of ladies' dresses, but their speciality was the 'pearl-fisher's jug', which was made from tin and had a glass bottom. The purpose of this object was to look for mussels in the river. Tinkers were expert beggars and were difficult to refuse because of what was described by one source as their 'adroitness in attack' and their 'whining appeal that would get through to all but the hardest of hearts'.

Not far from Laggan Bridge is a place called Balgowan, where there is a farm and a few crofts. Alaistair and Beryl MacRae live in one of a row of what used to be poor-houses. I spent an afternoon chatting about these dwellings to Alaistair, whose tales are from the recent past, only two generations ago. Paupers in those days, I discovered, were not down-and-outs. Often, Alaistair told me, the majority of people who landed in the paupers' houses were those who had worked hard all their lives, many of them on local estates. These estate workers had always lived in tied houses, but before the First World War retirement could be very difficult for old retainers, as they had little money to exist on and nowhere to live. There was no state pension and the poor were dependent on Parish Relief. At that time it was the job of the district inspector of the poor to allocate allowances from parish funds to the many needy and to offer to a fortunate few the paupers' houses as they became vacant. Each of these basic dwellings was occupied by a single person with his or her meagre possessions, but all shared the same outside lavatories and the same water standpipe at the far end of the row. The two rooms of each house had earth or stone floors, a large open fireplace where all food was cooked in black pots, and minimal furnishings. All was suitably organised and there was even a lady caretaker who lived in a room at the end of the houses to ensure that everything was kept in order.

A comparison of the exterior of these houses today with old photographs would show them to look remarkably similar, but inside they are very different. They are now comfortable, highly desirable properties. These charming cottages are particularly sought-after by those who long to leave busy cities in favour of the 'good life' in the country, especially in the beautiful and peaceful Highlands of Scotland.

4

A Small Hollow

THE translation for the Gaelic place-name Laggan is 'a small hollow' and on a clear day this little village at the far end of the Spey valley can be seen from the Torr, which is a hillock near the graveyard at Glentruim. From this vantage point there is also a good view across the Spey to Lochan Ovie, with the rocks of Creag Dubh rising up beyond. There are little hills all around, interrupted occasionally by clumps of birch trees, a perfect place for fairy knolls, which are reputed to be all over the Highlands.

By one of these knolls, according to legend, there have been occasional sightings of the Caillich Rua, a haggard old lady with red hair. In her youth, she fell in love with a young man whose family had unresolved grievances with her own, bad blood which eventually led to a fight between her brother and lover. Her brother, being reluctant to hurt his opponent, did not fight well and was killed. The Caillich Rua was so heart-broken that she never spoke again, and never returned home. Her spirit dashed, she wandered aimlessly through the valley, mourning her loss, often to be seen quietly walking through damp moss before she vanished into the surrounding woods. She knew full well that her brother had murdered her lover and although she did not want him punished, she resented the fact that no atonement was ever made for this injustice. No one could be sure whether she was dead or not, but her presence, whether human or ghostly, was very disturbing for the local people.

A local minister once decided to hold an open-air service beside Lochan Ovie, the location primarily chosen so that he could combine his two parishes for the forthcoming Sunday's celebrations. The proceedings were spectacular and well-attended, the hymns sung so heartily that they echoed off the black face of Creag Dubh. Many suspected that the minister had held the service there for the sole purpose of sanctifying the ground, so that the Caillich Rua's spirit could finally be at rest. Others, however, thought the notion very unlikely, for he had often warned his flock against superstition. He had told them that such beliefs were ungodly and that they should not allow themselves to think of diabolical manifestations such as the Caillich Rua. For all that, he was rather proud to discover that his followers truly thought he had the power to rid them of this heathen apparition, for it was never seen again. After it was pointed out to him that because he had been seen to liberate the spirit of the Caillich Rua, he too must have thought her presence credible in the first place. He was embarrassed by such a supposition and from that day onwards went out of his way to avoid the subject.

In those days it was often the case that services were shared between the two parishes, for Laggan did not have its own kirk until much later. In the 1770s, the local minister tried hard to persuade the duke of Gordon to build him a proper church, instead of the turf hut in which services were of necessity held. The minister at that time was a tall, powerful man, who was known to 'baptise at a distance', because of the physical gap between him and those that he wished to baptise. He achieved this notable feat by flinging the holy water across the river!

In approximately 1780 an imposing manse was built in Laggan, but before this the minister rented Drumgask farm, on the far bank of the Spey. According to an old tale, no sooner had he moved into the new manse than the farm was taken over by a new tenant, who made agricultural decisions that displeased him. The farmer wished to sow seed in a certain field considered unsuitable by the minister, who tried to dissuade him. However, the law was on the side of the farmer, so when the day came for sowing and the minister duly interfered, the sheriff officer and two of his men had to intervene. Although the minister was an elderly man with a long white beard, the sheriff treated him very badly, pulling his beard and tearing handfuls of hair out of it. One of the other officers was also brutal, nearly strangling the poor old man, whereas the third man stood back and pleaded with them to stop. When the minister's wife arrived on the scene, the brawling ceased and the minister, exhausted and in great pain, turned to the officer and said, 'I call Heaven to witness how you and that man have treated me today. Remember, all who hear me, I will not live to see it, but neither of these men will die a natural death. For you, my friend who pled for me, good will follow you.'

A few years later, after the minister had died, the man who had nearly strangled him was found dying at the side of the road near Pitmain, with his skull fractured and his face gouged. The sheriff also departed in strange circumstances: as he was stunning a bull for the butcher, he suddenly felt unwell, lay down beside the animal and died. The third man, who had pleaded on behalf of the minister, was spared and lived on to tell the tale.

Catlodge, the estate where the famous piper Calum Piobair lived after leaving Cluny, is situated behind Gasbeg. The Lodge itself is reputed to be haunted, which is not surprising, considering that the earliest part of the building, the west end, dates back to 1640 and was originally an old courthouse, where men were tried and sentenced to death for theft, mainly of livestock. They were hanged across the road from Catlodge on Gallowshill. Richard Miller, the current owner of Catlodge, is convinced that the old part of the house is haunted, for he and some of his house-guests have experienced sightings. He told me that there is a particular spot in the downstairs corridor, where two passages cross, that is sometimes icy cold. Whenever they are at this spot, the family dogs bark, stare and if need be scout round whatever seems to be standing in their way. We had just such a spot at Glentruim in the top corridor: our dogs too refused to enter the lower half and if we forced them, they bounded through as if their lives depended on getting to the other end. Close by that sinister part of Catlodge is a staircase to the servants' quarters and it was there that Richard once saw someone he thought was a chamber maid, dressed in black with a white pinafore, climbing the stairs. He shouted 'Hello!' as he followed her up to the second floor, but when he got to the top, she had gone. Her skirt has often been heard rustling on those stairs. He also claims that there is a poltergeist in the house, for on another occasion Richard lost his glasses, looked everywhere for them and finally found them on a couch he had been sitting on the day before, in a room that he had thoroughly searched before securely locking the door. Further proof of the presence of a poltergeist came when he went into another locked room to wind the grandfather clock, as he always did on a Sunday morning, only to find that it had already been done for him!

In addition, Cluny of the '45 is said to haunt the east end of the house. He was involved in the uprising of 1745 and having been a fugitive on his own estate for nine years, he took flight across the Spey to Catlodge, whence he watched his castle being burnt down by his pursuers. His ghost is said to frighten any Sassenach who sleeps in a certain bedroom, causing them to awake screaming, allegedly with marks on the neck from the grip of Cluny's hands.

For most of his time in hiding, Cluny lived behind a wooded precipice on Creag Dubh, where his men dug a cave for him, depositing the waste material into Lochan Ovie. This refuge was so well-hidden behind the trees that when the mist came down, as it often did, not even the cliff-edge could be seen. The *Kingussie Record* once reported that, 'Creag Dubh serves as a kind of district barometer, for whenever it assumes a cap of mist, it is popularly believed that a storm is not far away!' As a fugitive, Cluny often made clandestine visits to his wife, who had been allowed to live in one of the estate cottages, where a secret recess in a wall enabled him to hide quickly if he was in danger. However, his best defence was the loyalty of his clansmen, who never divulged his whereabouts, even with a £1,000 reward on his head.

Cluny Castle was later rebuilt by Cluny's only son, Duncan of the Kiln, and in the nineteenth century it was nearly always rented out. Indeed, Andrew Carnegie, the famous philanthropist, rented it for ten years, a time that Mrs Carnegie described as the golden period of her married life. They chose Cluny Castle after falling in love with the bagpipes! Carnegie had been invited to lay the foundation stone of the Edinburgh Carnegie Free Library, which he generously donated to the city. There were pipes at the ceremony and, totally enchanted by the music, Mrs Carnegie asked her husband if they could have their own piper. He agreed, so they put advertisements in the newspapers and interviewed many pipers, one of whom was John Macpherson, son of Malcolm Macpherson, the famous piper. He arrived at their Scottish summer house with glowing references from Cluny Macpherson and was immediately offered the post. The house they initially rented was Kilgraston, which belonged to the Grant family, in Bridge of Earn, Perthshire. In later years this became a private boarding school for girls.

Kilgraston proved inadequate for their requirements, so they started to look for a larger house to take each summer. It was at John Macpherson's suggestion that they rented Cluny Castle and they returned year after year. John was pleased to be back in his homeland, surrounded by his family again. The Carnegies had fallen in love with Cluny and would readily have bought it, but it was not for sale at the time they required it, for a son of Old Cluny was to be married and planned to live there. Although this was a big disappointment to the Carnegies, they eventually found an ideal place further north, Skibo Castle, which they enjoyed for many years. The area thus lost very valuable members of the community, for the Carnegies were well-respected, particularly for their benevolence towards the local people. It is said that Andrew Carnegie would visit all the crofters once a year, sit the children on his knee and give them a gold sovereign, which, as the equivalent of a year's pay, was enough to buy all the school clothes and boots a child might need until his next visit. He was indeed a generous man.

Kilgraston, incidentally, became a Convent of the Sacred Heart and was the school that my sister and I attended. It has changed a great deal since we were there, having grown out of all recognition, and whereas most lessons used to be taught by nuns clad in habits and wimples, nowadays there are lay teachers as well. Some of the nuns were very strict and serious, but others were fun. I fondly recall the young nun who taught us tennis and hockey, who rolled up her long robe, then enthusiastically joined in the game. When I was given my first car, I tried to teach her to drive in the grounds of Kilgraston, but gave up after she reversed into a tree. She was a friend I was to keep long after I left school, when her nun's robes were later exchanged for ordinary women's fashion.

We were groomed to be ladies, etiquette and deportment being paramount. I once came across an interesting advertisement in a local newspaper from the 1920s, promoting a shoe shop in Kingussie: 'A graceful carriage is the result of being properly shod. The desire of every woman is to be graceful, yet how many have yet to learn that a graceful walk depends almost entirely upon choosing shoes that fit the foot correctly – supporting where support is needed, flexing with caressing snugness as the feet flex in walking.' Our school shoes were never referred to in this way, but they did have to be well-polished. We were brought up to have substance, and during my time at Glentruim, I certainly needed it and hard work was inevitable. Striding forward undaunted from one venture to the next, I knew well how difficult it was for others coming into the valley to make a living.

A few years after we arrived at Glentruim, a couple called Mick Arnold and Lynda Whitty decided to move into a semi-derelict building on the Catlodge estate early one January. Despite the lack of running water and freezing indoor temperatures, they somehow managed to camp there for over six months. Water had to be fetched from the houses of obliging neighbours, a local farmer's wife kindly did their washing and milk-churns served as legs for their plywood table, for want of any proper furniture. Despite the difficulties and discomfort, it was an adventure, for they were young and extremely enthusiastic: primitive conditions posed an exciting challenge. Having worked for a few years in a pottery in Comrie, Lynda was both qualified and ready to start her own business.

Jimmy the postie was the last occupant of the small water-tight part of the house, which had a cement floor and which he had used mainly as a workshop. It had also served as the Laggan Cinema, the best seats being old deck-chairs! Jimmy would get the generator going, then put on films for his audience. I remember a similar arrangement in my own childhood days, when films were organised in a freezing cold village hall, and smoke from cigarettes and pipes clouded the view of the screen.

The first time that Mick and Lynda went out for a drink locally they visited the Gaskmore House Hotel, across the river at the other side of Laggan. Alastair Thomson, the owner and a fine figure of a man, was in his kilt behind the bar that evening and Lynda, recalling her struggles during the day as she battled against the elements, remembers thinking to herself, 'What *have* I come to?' Strangely enough, I think I felt the same when Euan and I visited the Gaskmore for the first time. I too must have had a difficult day and I must also have stood in the way of the dartboard, because my evening ended with a dart sticking out of my head! The night the Gaskmore House Hotel caught fire was a shock for us all round Laggan. Mick went out into the garden early in the evening and thought that mist had come down, lying low in the valley. About eight o' clock, the sirens of fire engines were heard and everyone realised what was happening. The hotel was burned to the ground, but luckily no one was injured.

As the years passed, the pottery that Lynda set up and named Caoldair has grown out of all recognition. She and Mick worked hard, gradually renovating and adapting their buildings for their expanding business. Lynda still runs the Caoldair Pottery, which has a tearoom with home-baking and a craft shop where her hand-thrown, wood-fired ceramics are sold, among other things. There is also a bunkhouse with a hot-tub spa at its front door. How delightful for visitors to sit in the warmth of the tub, surrounded by spectacular scenery! Such luxury is quite a contrast to the less-than-basic facilities available to the young couple when they first arrived in Laggan.

I can imagine Lynda's former existence amid the dilapidation in her new abode all too well, for our home at Glentruim involved a certain amount of predictable discomfort. There could be long periods without water, both in winter and summer. The pipes might be frozen up for many days before the ice thawed, after which the dreaded bursts caused even more problems, sometimes bringing ceilings down. It was equally tiresome when the water-tanks dried out in times of drought, although at least we were warm. Our water then had to be fetched from the village or, as happened on a couple of occasions, the fire brigade came and filled the tanks.

Fine old houses in splendid isolation always tend to have their drawbacks, particularly when some of the public services are lacking, but they often also have the inestimable advantage of tranquillity and stunning views, such as we enjoyed in the heart of Badenoch and Strathspey.

5

The Raeburn Hut

THE cottage we knew as Halfway House (part of the Glentruim estate) used, for a short time previously, to be known as Burnside Cottage. Now its front door clearly shows that it has been renamed Raeburn. Strategically placed between Dalwhinnie and Laggan, the Raeburn Hut stands alone at the side of the road. There tranquillity reigns. Running water from a stream at the edge of the other side of the road was the only sound to break the silence when we were at Glentruim. A cluster of birch trees still stands behind the dwelling, not thick enough to give shelter, but beautifully placed to furnish an artist's dream. Dalwhinnie, to the south, has been described as the only place of historical interest in a bleak and cheerless glen because, in 1745, Sir John Cope held a council of war there. However, this sleepy little Highland village would have been busy in the days when it had a cattle stance, being constantly used as a stopping place en route to auctions further south. The drovers could get free ale, accommodation and hospitality at the government's expense in the King's House, later called the Loch Ericht Hotel. When the hotel became more tourist-orientated in the mid-1990s, there were advertisements in the newspapers stating that this place was 'on the roof of Scotland (1,200 ft. alt), ideal for Health, Air, Scenery'! Also offered was 'pleasure sailing on Loch Ericht in comfortable motor launch'. In those early days of motor boats, it seems to

41

have been quite newsworthy when motor launches broke down and anglers had to be towed back, even if they returned safely.

Not far from the Raeburn Hut is Loch Caoldair, which was not such a lucky fishing haunt for Malcolm Macpherson, better known as Callum Piobair. Malcolm loved to fish and this was one of his favourite places, but during one of his expeditions there, his boat capsized. Although Callum was pulled out of the water and taken straight to the nearest shelter, which was Halfway House, he tragically died there only two days later.

Callum Piobair had lived near Halfway House, in a cottage at Catlodge, just before the turning to Glentruim. His piping was legendary and, amongst many others, he taught John MacDonald, another famous piper, who was born on the Glentruim Estate and whose father was piper to Macpherson of Glentruim, my late husband's family. Because of Callum's influence, Badenoch has made its mark in the piping world, particularly for solo pipers. Many pipe tunes are dedicated to chiefs, chieftains and other notable people and places. There are particular Glentruim tunes, such as 'The Ball of Glentruim' and the 'Hills of Glentruim March'. Whether they were composed to honour the name of the laird or his estate is immaterial, Glentruim being the heritable title of that branch of the Macphersons as well as the name of their estate.

By the early nineteenth century the great age of pipe composition was dwindling. Fortunately, we have had additions to the dance music tradition since then, which include a Strathspey, 'The Macphersons of Edinburgh', and the reel 'Lady Stewart Macpherson'. I was privileged to know Lady Stewart Macpherson, who died in 1976 when she was 101. She was remarkable. I recall her taking great command over family lunches, sitting at the top of the table with her middle-aged children, grand-children and great-grand-children all around her. She was still very much head of the family, with an outstandingly sharp mind even in her later years.

Dr Kenneth Mackay, the local doctor, who had retired by the time we went to live at Glentruim, was also a great piper, teacher and judge of the pibroch. He started the Laggan school of piping and under his instruction his pupils practised on hillsides and moors around the area. Dr Mackay organised the erection of a monument in memory of Callum Piobair.

★★★

I believe that in the nineteenth and early twentieth centuries it was mostly professional people who climbed mountains, for they had the time and the ability to get around the country under their own steam. Those who did not have their own means of transport would take the train to Dalwhinnie, then cycle to either Fort William or over to Laggan to carry out their climbs, and would cycle back again in the evening, such was their enthusiasm. Then, during the Depression, fine climbers from the working class, as it was called then, came on the scene. In the 1930s, apparently, many of the Creag Dubh climbers were out of work, many from the industrial belt of Scotland, and certainly some from the Clyde shipyards in particular.

Near Laggan you will find Craig Meagaidh, which has the second biggest cliff after Ben Nevis. The rock-climbing is usually considered tricky there because of the scree on the face, but in the winter, when such debris is covered by ice, it provides a good climb, the first of which was made in 1896. Gerry Peet of the Scottish Mountaineering Club (SMC), a keen climber for a great many years, enthusiastically told me about his favourite mountains and ascents. From him I learned that the various routes up Craig Meagaidh have unusual names such as The Pumpkin, Cinderella, The Ugly Sister, The Glass Slipper and The Fairy Godmother. It was also common in the nineteenth century for climbs to be given the names of those who discovered them. 'That is now frowned upon, and has resulted in new names being very much tongue-in-cheek,' said Gerry. 'For instance, when taking a steep ice-route in direct line up the left flank of Bellevue Buttress on Creag Meagaidh, there is a "Naevueata", (Nae-view-at-a') and close to this one is "Lotsavu"!' He spelled these names for me first, in order not to spoil the fun!

At Glentruim we often used to hear helicopters circling around, looking for the injured on Creag Dubh (which means The Black Rock), which was just across the River Spey from the estate. Gerry told me that numerous rescues had been made on this mountain, but he also remembered one fatality on Creag Meagaidh. He recalled, 'Two men were climbing, then, having finished the climb, had unroped. One stepped back, tripped over the rope and fell down the rock-face off the pinnacle buttress. The climber who died was the twin brother of the other climber, who still climbs to this today.' 'Creag Dubh' was clan at the end of the Clan March in the Eilean, in Newtonmore, at our annual gathering.

There are fewer fatalities on the mountains these days because of better equipment, and also because of efficient modern clothing. In the early years of climbing it was not recognised that wool and silk absorbed moisture and therefore there was a greater risk of hypothermia. Now, with modern fibres such as Gortex and fleece, both being 'wicking' fabrics, moisture is drawn into the atmosphere, leaving the climber dry.

Climbing stories are not always just about the sport; they sometimes concern strange happenings. In the 1950s, certain members of the Edinburgh University Mountaineering Club spent a New Year at Ben Alder Cottage, a two-roomed bothy not far from the south end of Loch Ericht, a popular base for ascending Ben Alder. A brief flurry of snow had covered the surrounding ground. The club members settled into their sleeping-bags in one of the rooms, but later that night they were disturbed by the sound of footsteps outside. They also thought that they heard someone walking round the other room in heavy boots. On investigation, no one was found in the second room and there were no footprints outside in the snow. When the group later told local people about their experience, they discovered that a gamekeeper had hanged himself in this bothy. Gerry told me that he and his climbing friends used to stay in this very place after the war, many years after the tragedy, but that they had heard nothing. Some time later one of them stayed there alone but, as Gerry told me, 'He was as deaf as a post, so he didn't hear a bloody thing!'

For some reason, people are drawn to hills and mountains in the same way that others are drawn to the sea. I can understand why climbers have a passion for their sport, whether for a risky rock-climb or to 'bag' another Munro, but for me the hills are quite simply home.

***

We sold Halfway House to the Scottish Mountaineering Club (SMC) in 1987. Before Gerry came to see us about it, we had thought that this solitary house would benefit from being regularly inhabited. Because it had begun to be frequented by squatters, a continuous stream of climbers staying there seemed to be the answer. It was too remote to be monitored all of the time and latterly, when the passing traffic began to increase, it began to have more and more unwelcome visitors. A survey revealed that the foundations had been lifted by the frost and the structure was damaged. The whole house was demolished and rebuilt to look exactly the same on the outside as before. The only part of the old property that remains is the little gate reinforced with mesh and this has been returned to me as a keepsake of the original Halfway House. It is such a different place inside now, modern and warm. With extra windows upstairs in the two dormitories, the stunning views across to the Monadhliath mountains can be enjoyed by all guests. The climbers sleep on Mattrezzenlager beds, which are shelves that provide a firm wooden base for mattresses. 'It is the sardine principle,' said Gerry, who is now the custodian of the hut. Mixed company, on communal shelves in sleeping bags does not seem to bother climbers. Pillows are not supplied, but in their absence rolled-up clothes make a good substitute. The house is kept much warmer now than in the old days, when open fires and paraffin lamps were relied upon to bring up the heat as quickly as possible. Now there is even a system where fan-heaters come on if the temperature drops below 4 degrees centigrade. What a luxury! But, I thought, as I walked through this place that I no longer knew, how sad to lose the large open fires; I had often sat beside them, watching the flames dancing higher and higher as I piled on the logs and peat to keep off the chill in an exceedingly cold place. It always smelt of damp, peat and paraffin. Whenever I smell peat burning, I always think of Halfway House. It was such a romantic place to be, so quietly picturesque, where the past could be glimpsed and where, perhaps, dreams could be realised.

The SMC named the hut after Harold Raeburn (1865–1926), who joined the club in 1896 and quickly made his mark as a bold and original climber, often years ahead of his time. This was the era of hob-nailed boots, tweed clothing and hemp rope. There are many gullies, buttresses and arêtes all over Scotland named after Harold, including Raeburn's Gully, Lochnagar 1898; Raeburn's Gully, Creag Meagaidh 1903, and Raeburn's Buttress, Ben Nevis 1908. Harold climbed Kanchenjunga in 1920 and was a member of the 1921 Everest reconnaissance expedition, but he became ill with dysentery and never really regained full health. He was considered a remarkable man, many of whose routes on Ben Nevis are still highly respected.

I asked Gerry whether there had been any strange occurrences since we sold the house, knowing that a tramp, a squatter there, had committed suicide by hanging himself from the banister during the mid-1970s. Only by chance had I decided not to go in with the children on the very day he was found dead by other squatters. I was firmly told by Gerry that there were no ghosts in the new Raeburn Hut. 'In any case,' he said, 'I don't believe in ghosts.'

However, Gerry did have a very interesting visitor the year after the dwelling was rebuilt. An old lady had appeared at the kitchen window and he welcomed her in.

'She was very lively and interested in the building,' he told me. 'She said, "I lived here before the war and it was a very happy place."' Hearing this, Gerry thought to himself that she had obviously not heard about the sad death of the tramp. 'We did not have all the facilities that you have today,' the old lady continued. 'There was no privy – our bathroom was God's!' The sky was her ceiling; in our time protection from the elements was provided by the low wooden roof of a lean-to, which accommodated a chemical loo. No convenience of a bathroom of any description for either of us!

I enquired how the old lady had arrived that day. 'Well, I never saw a car, no form of transport as far as I remember,' said Gerry. 'She arrived and she left, with no sight or sound of a vehicle.' 'Was that not strange?' I asked Gerry. He had not given it a thought, for he had been busy fire-proofing the kitchen ceiling and was eager to get back to work. She was just an old lady who had visited and they had had a fascinating chat. He was confident that she had lived for a long time at Halfway House and had tried to work out the age she would have been, presuming that it was Elizabeth Macpherson.

Elizabeth Macpherson and her husband, Ian, were both teachers and had dropped out of their demanding roles in Aberdeen to become hawkers. They lived for a while at Halfway House and wrote about their adventures: *The Happy Hawkers*, a copy of which I had found in a corner cupboard in the dining-room of Halfway House, signed by Ian, describes their happiest times in the little house they rented from the Glentruim estate. I still have that cupboard and their books in my own house today and I treasure them all. They describe contented, carefree days, when they gathered tales from one side of Strathspey and Badenoch to the other and made a living out of hawking.

Ian and Elizabeth published their works in the late 1930s. They would probably have been in their thirties when they lived at Halfway House and Elizabeth would have been well into her eighties when visiting the Raeburn Hut. It is possible that it could have been she herself, but what was her means of transport on the very remote road that runs over the hill that links Laggan to Dalwhinnie?

I discovered that one of Ian and Elizabeth's daughters, Jane, lived in Forres and that her sister lived south of the border. I visited Jane on a hot spring day. Travelling across Dava Moor was a joy, with the the roof of the car down, a glow of warmth and brisk, fresh Scottish air. I was pleased to find Jane's sister, Elizabeth, also there that afternoon.

Elizabeth and Jane talked fondly of their parents and had been busy compiling a book in their memory. Their father was tragically killed on his motor-bike in 1944. He was only thirty-eight and the girls were very young. Elizabeth continued to write after her husband's death and in the mid-1940s some of her more memorable pieces appeared in one of Scotland's tabloids of the day, *The Bulletin*. The articles were part of a series entitled 'Leaning on a Gate'. They were gentle stories of simple country life; whether they told of days in the cornfields, picking tatties or dealing with livestock, they were all enchanting. While I was with her daughters, the eldest, who bore her mother's name, told me of an episode she remembered from her days working in a Grantown boarding-house as a teenager. While she was serving lunch, the nephew of the lady of the house, an engineer from Aberdeen, asked her, 'Are you Elizabeth and Ian Macpherson's daughter?' When she revealed that she was, he told her of the time he had met her father.

The gentleman had been working on the old A9 and Ian Macpherson was running a taxi business. The usual pleasantries were exchanged and then Ian asked, 'How's it going?'

'Not very well. We have come to a huge rock and we have run out of dynamite.'

'Och, that's alright,' chirped Ian, 'I have dynamite back at Halfway House.'

Elizabeth was somewhat shocked at this statement and wondered whether it was true, so when she got home that night she quizzed her mother, who promptly said, 'Yes, that is quite right. It was kept under the bed.' Her mother's reply was so calm, it sounded as if was quite normal to keep dynamite under the bed. 'I would not like to think what Father was up to with the dynamite, but one could have a good guess!' Elizabeth said to me after telling this tale. We had just been talking about undesirable ways of catching salmon!

Elizabeth Macpherson died in 1989, the year after Halfway House was rebuilt. It would be nice to think that she had been the mysterious elderly lady who visited the Raeburn Hut that day. This but and ben had been a primitive home, a rendezvous for shooting parties, a house where some ended their lives, and where others longed to return. Halfway House enjoyed 'happy hawkers' for much of its life and now, with any luck, the Raeburn Hut will be blessed with happy climbers for many years to come.

6

The Spectre

IT would be more usual to see the Brocken Spectre in the Alps, yet this phenomenon has sometimes been experienced in the Highlands of Scotland. In order to see the Brocken there has to be both sunshine and mist on the mountain. It is said that the right condition for this apparition is when a corrie (mountain hollow) is covered with mist and sunshine seeps through from above. If you stand on the edge of a deep corrie, with the sun peering from behind and thick mist below, there is a chance of seeing your own gigantic shadow looking down on you from a distant hill on the other side. At the same time, if someone were standing beside you, there could be a second shadow alongside your own. Yet if either of you were to move just an inch, the shadows could disappear. Then again, if one of you moved in another direction, you might find both your shadows on another hilltop or corrie edge. It is an eerie experience, but perhaps the legends of giants in the mountains could be explained by this strange occurrence.

Ben Macdhui is the highest mountain in the Cairngorm range and it has the reputation of being haunted. The majority of climbers who have tackled the Cairngorms over the years have either heard of or encountered the Fear Liath Mor (Ferla Mhor), which means the Big Grey Man. This figure is said to haunt the Lairig Ghru, the great defile that cuts through the mountains, as well as Ben Macdhui itself, which rises from its eastern wall. According to Affleck Gray, who wrote about 'The Big Grey Man of Ben Macdhui', there does exist 'a strange influence which is wholly inimical and apart from this world'. It has been said that no other mountain in Britain can boast such a large number of weird and uncanny experiences. The strange happenings include sightings of a figure dragging heavy chains, a huge beast with talons and strange footprints in the snow. Voices, ghostly music and the sound of footsteps have also been reported.

A reputable witness to this sinister manifestation, described by Affleck as one of the greatest climbers of his generation, was a Professor Norman Collie from Aberdeen. His story is one of 'stark terror on Ben Macdhui'. The professor actually confessed his fear publicly to the Cairngorm Club in Aberdeen in the early twentieth century. What he said to his audience was this: 'I was returning from the cairn on the summit in a mist when I began to think I heard something else than merely the noise of my own footsteps. For every few steps I took I heard a crunch, and then another crunch as if someone was walking after me but taking steps three or four times the length of my own. I said to myself, "This is all nonsense." I heard it again, but could see nothing in the mist. As I walked on and the eerie crunch, crunch, sounded behind me, I was seized with terror and took to my heels, staggering blindly among the boulders for four or five miles nearly down to Rothiemurchus Forest. Whatever you make of it I do not know, but there is something very queer about the top of Ben Macdhui and I will not go back there again myself, I know.' Collie also admitted that when he stopped running and reached the edge of the corrie, he had a strong urge to throw himself over.

Dr A.M. Kellas, another great climber of the last century, also witnessed the Brocken Spectre, although he was loath to admit it. This encounter, reported in the 1920s in the Aberdeen *Press and Journal* by W.G. Robertson, occurred when Dr Kellas and his brother were chipping for crystals on rocks in the Cairngorm mountains. The atmospheric conditions were exactly as previously mentioned, but on this particular day the two brothers saw only one giant figure coming towards them. They subsequently fled in fear down the mountain, knowing full well that they were being followed closely by this gigantic apparition. They did not, however, hear any footsteps behind them. Because there had been only a single shadow, they did not believe that it could have been an optical illusion. If this had been the case then, according to the brothers, there should have been another shadow.

Alistair Borthwick's classic *Always a Little Further*, which is about the Scottish hills, relates stories of the Big Grey Man, noting that ' the local people will not talk of the creature'. Today the villagers are only too willing to talk about the Big Grey Man, and those whose ancestors have experienced this spectre are proud to tell the tale. On the other hand, there have also been some who were intrigued and even amused to encounter the Brocken Spectre, such as A.G. Duthie and his friend. One hot day they were climbing above the corrie on Lochnagar, which was covered in deep snow, when, having struggled long enough with their ice axes, they decided to stop for a rest. There was thick snow to be seen for miles across the peaks and as they looked down into the mist-filled corrie, they saw their own enormous shadows. This unexpected sight made them momentarily speechless, but they were not frightened. On the contrary, they played games with their eerie shadows, moving about in the snow and taking up different positions as they watched their huge dopplegangers jump from hill to hill across the other side of the corrie.

Duthie had another interesting experience after climbing Ben Macdhui one day. As he was making his way back over the Lairig Ghru and approaching the vicinity of the Courrour Bothy, he thought that he heard the sound of bagpipes. It was 'a long, stately tune like a pibroch or a lament', he wrote. However, when he reached the hut and entered, there was no piper, but when he set off again, 'the sound of the pipes returned until the haunting strains of the tune faded away into the gloaming of the fast descending night'. Many years previously there had been a piper who used to play in this hut to pass the time away while watching the deer. Perhaps it was his spirit that played on!

Another very interesting and different witness account is that of Sir Hugh Rys Rankin, a Mahayana Buddhist and former vice-president of the Scottish National Liberal Association, as well as former president of the Rough Stuff Cycling Association. He wrote an article in the local newspaper about his experience while venturing through the Lairig Ghru in the Cairngorms in the late 1960s. As they walked along, he and his wife (also a Buddhist) saw a vision of what they believed to be the bodhisattva. This, according to Buddhist authorities, is the 'perfect man'. The ethereal embodiment was accompanied by what sounded like the music of the pipes carried in a very strong wind, according to Sir Hugh. He mentioned that if the locals had experienced the same thing, they might have thought that they had seen the Grey Man of Ben Macdhui! Under the heading of 'The Abominable Snowman', Sir Hugh also wrote to the editor of the *Glasgow Herald* in 1960, stating that 'No expedition in future taken by any country, at any time, in order to find or capture or kill the Himalayan "Abominable Snowman" will ever be successful. He cannot be killed or captured or wounded as he is a Buddhist celestial being, one of the five Buddhist bodhisattvas who control the destinies of this world. He lives in the Himalayas. One of the five bodhisattvas lives in the Scottish Cairngorms.' Could this also be our Grey Man, I wonder? Whatever the speculative attempts to explain away the Grey Man, the Abominable Snowman or any other spectre said to lurk in the Highlands, too many sightings have been recorded for them to be ignored. Some, moreover, have occurred in the recent past.

In the early twentieth century a stalker called Kennedy, who worked at Drumochter Lodge near Dalwhinnie, was out on the Boar of Badenoch, a conical hill above the Drumochter Pass. There, he too witnessed the Brocken Spectre. At the time he was stalking with a well-known author, Henry Tegner, who also saw the apparition of two large figures travelling at great speed across the brow of the Boar. The figures stopped as if to look at them, then vanished out of sight. It was an extraordinary experience for them both. 'Certainly uncanny, and sent shivers down my spine,' Kennedy is known to have admitted. This was not all that Kennedy experienced during his years in those parts, for one early July evening in 1908 he claimed to have seen a brilliant flare, fanning out like the rays of the sun to a vast height in the sky, caused by volcanic dust erupting from Mount Hekla in Iceland. For two or three nights the darkness in Drumochter was obliterated by this bright light, or so he said!

There is an amusing tale about the time when Kennedy first came to take up his post at Drumochter Lodge, in 1888. Having been successful in his application for a stalker's job, he had travelled by train with his wife and family (a boy, two girls and a dog), and all his worldly goods. Arriving at Dalwhinnie station, Kennedy borrowed a wheelbarrow from the station master, loaded it with the bare necessities, then made his way to the Lodge with his family. The next day he went back to the railway station to ask the station master if he could store his remaining belongings for him because, as he said, 'I don't intend to stay in that terrible place.' The station master tended to agree with his sentiment.Over the next few weeks the locals noticed that wheelbarrow-loads of belongings were being pushed along by Kennedy in the direction of the Lodge, so they presumed that he had decided to stay. He had indeed, and the family lived there for forty-five years!

Kennedy was trim in his appearance, and those who knew him remembered him for his pointed white 'Captain Kettle' beard.

For that reason he was known by the so-called 'toffs' as Beardie, but the locals affectionately called him Pharaoh. When Kennedy retired in 1933, he moved to Newtonmore and happened to land next door to Joseph McCook, who had formerly lived at Ben Alder Cottage, Ben Alder being the estate adjoining Drumochter, on the other side of Loch Ericht from Dalwhinnie. How bizarre that they had worked as neighbours, then by chance retired as such.

A railway bridge south of Balsporan was named 'Beardie's Bridge' after Kennedy, and he and his wife were buried in Laggan Bridge graveyard. Kennedy died at the age of 79, his wife at 101. Old Kennedy's grandson, who recently talked to me about his grandfather, said that he often wondered whether his grandmother had ever thought in her latter years of her husband's words the day they arrived at Dalwhinnie: 'We will not stay in this terrible place.'

Dalwhinnie was described as a bleak place by Queen Victoria and I remember thinking it was particularly so when returning one winter's day from Edinburgh by rail in the early 1970s. Snow had been falling continuously since dawn, and not only was it lying but the wind was scooping it up, causing drifts that increased in size by the minute. Visibility had also become poor. As the train approached Drumochter Pass, the highest point through the mountains, where snow had obliterated the whole landscape, I strained my eyes to see if I could spot any sign of life at all through the windows of the train, but saw only the wild, treacherous blizzard being driven in our direction. The train began to slow and eventually stopped about half a mile from Dalwhinnie station. Thick snow lay high over the railway line in front of us and we were stranded. It was not long before there was neither light nor heating on the train, and it was freezing. I could not have imagined being stuck in snow-drifts in a worse place, given the isolation of Dalwhinnie. Even if we could have trudged the last half mile by foot, we would have been lucky to find assistance. The road over to Glentruim via the back road to Laggan would certainly have been closed and the snow-gates shut, as would those on the old A9.

I cannot recall how long we were marooned in the train that night. Frozen to the marrow and with nothing much to eat or drink, our plight was far worse than that of Queen Victoria, who complained that she had been given as supper only 'meagre starved chickens' during a visit to Dalwhinnie. For a brief moment, I too thought that it was a terrible place, but eventually the track was cleared and we began to move again. Although it was dark, I knew that we were not far across the hill from that 'happy place', Halfway House. I sighed with relief as I spotted Glentruim, my haven, on our final lap of the journey to Newtonmore.

***

As far back as the time of the Rebellion of 1745, there were tales of other kinds of ghostly happenings at Drumochter. Prince Charlie was taking his troops through Badenoch and had intended that they should rest awhile over Drumochter. Being staunch warriors, the McPherson and MacDonald regiments were eager to make an attack on the enemy and marched forward regardless of their orders, typical of such strong-minded clans. In preparation for the expected onslaught, the English had made a deep trench with high boulders piled up on one side to barricade themselves against the opposing armies of clansmen. In true Highland style the Scottish regiments fought fiercely, and the English began to fall. With little difficulty the two clans clambered over the boulders into the trenches and slaughtered many men. Those who escaped were given chase on horseback and the Highlanders were satisfied only when every single member of the enemy had been slain. It was on the banks of Ault-na-Sasunnach, The Englishman's Burn, that the last of the English were killed. Later a stone was erected at the side of the burn to commemorate that day. It is said that if one wanders into the area of the battlefield around twilight, bagpipe music can be heard, as well as other very strange noises, and the phantoms of fighting soldiers are sometimes seen in the dimness.

Disturbing spectral occurrences were often left in the wake of Highland battles such as the Battle of Invernahavon, which was fought in the fields below Glentruim in the fourteenth century. The ghosts of the warriors who once strode towards that bloody clash marched through our bedroom at Glentruim in the 1970s, just as they had in the fourteenth century. Their piper was also still to be heard piping in those nearby fields, as he had so many years before during the battle, but only from the old servant's quarters. I was told by cooks and housemaids that they had been kept awake by the sound of pipes, but initially I dismissed their tales, regarding them as figments of wild imagination, brought on by village gossip. Normally we advertised in the South for our resident staff, on the assumption they would have no preconceived ideas about haunted houses. It had always been difficult to hire local girls because they were far too frightened by stories of ghosts and poltergeists to come to live at Glentruim. These old buildings generated fear of the unknown, their creaks and groans tending to stimulate the wildest tales of superstition and the occult. I knew this all too well, having been subject to such fears when I first arrived at Glentruim, for there were indeed unexplained happenings.

Euan, who personally had never believed in ghosts, at least not until our children started making certain reports, did mention to me a phantom butler who was reputed to roam the house. There had always been such a retainer before we inherited the place and always barrels full of whisky in the cellars below which required decanting, so I suspect he was the result of mere wishful thinking! I am sure a good few stories derived from the delivery of the barrels and the consumption of the whisky at Glentruim, given the convenient proximity of the distillery at Dalwhinnie.

There are far more tangible, natural phenomena and hazards

to be worried about in remote places, for instance blizzards and thunderstorms, which can terrify people and drive them off high mountain tops such as the Cairngorms. A.G. Duthie wrote of an occasion on these hills when the heavens opened 'in a terrific and deafening barrage of thunder'. Lightning was striking the mountainside and the intervals between lightning and thunder were short, which meant the storm was almost immediately over-head. He said that he could feel the electricity in the ground through his hobnailed boots.

Only once did I experience such terror in an electric storm. I was alone in the house at Glentruim one warm sultry afternoon. There was not a sound in the air, for the birds had stopped chirping in the grounds and even my peacocks had gone quiet, unusual for them during the summer months. The stillness was ominous. In an instant I knew that something was about to happen, and it did. Thunderclaps rent the air with such force that I felt the very walls of the massive granite building shudder; strong though they were, the storm had found their weak points. At the same time came the lightning, streaking across the shiny linoleum in the front hall in one big crackling flash, only stopping when it reached the far wall. I could smell sparks from the lightning and was motionless, too frightened to step across the room in case it struck again. Rooted there, I waited until the interval between noise and light lengthened, then I ventured towards the nearest telephone, but I found that the lines were down. There was no help at hand, so I had no choice but to wait patiently for the storm to cease. Both fear and curiosity forced me to sit on the floor for over an hour at the edge of the hall, not daring to go elsewhere, too mesmerised to allow this uncon-trollable event of nature to pass without watching. At least I was at home that day, but how terrifying to be as exposed to lightning flashes as on top of a mountain.

The beauty of the wild countryside, the imposing mountains amid peace and solitude, outweighs any hint of mythical creatures or danger through inclement weather for those who choose to live there. Indeed, in a place so full of legends and history one expects to find traces of such things; perhaps it would be disappointing if this were not the case. After all, would life not be rather dull if we knew what was around the corner?

7

The Airstrip

IN 1965 Denny Wilson, the art master at the High School in Kingussie, approached Bill Longstaff, the local dentist, with whom he had previously discussed gliding and flying, asking him if he would be interested in starting a gliding club. He also placed an advertisement in the *Badenoch and Strathspey Herald* and when Bill Macdonald of Blackmill Farm, Kincraig, responded to this a few days later, Denny arrived at his door with the same question. Bill Macdonald had previous experience of teaching air cadets in Inverness, and another respondent, Sandy Lindsay, had flown Spitfires as a pilot in the RAF during the Second World War, later instructing in Harvards. The founder members of the proposed club soon met at Pormoak, Kinross, for some training.

By late 1966 the Cairngorm Gliding Club had been officially founded at Feshiebridge (better known as Feshie), with a membership of ten men and their wives, each contributing a mere £50. Denny, Bill Macdonald, Mike Waller and Sandy Lindsay were all experienced pilots, but the other six were total beginners.

Different areas were looked at for suitability, but eventually a strip of moorland scrub owned by Jane Williamson, whose farm manager was Bill Macdonald, was chosen. Later Jane's brother, Fergus, bought two and a half acres of land from the Forestry Commission to increase the length of the airfield. This site is surrounded by quite the most beautiful scenery that anyone in a glider could wish for, for the strath in which it lies contains rich pasture interspersed with belts of evergreens, and lochs bordered by neat little houses. Over all loom the high Monadhliath and Cairngorm mountains, with the steep face of Craig Mhigeachaidh sitting only half a mile away from the edge of the airstrip.

The beautiful River Feshie was once described by Queen Victoria as 'a fine, rapid river, full of stones'. Its source is in the Grampians at the watershed between Blair Athol and Speyside, but it is joined by a large tributary, the Eidart, from the Cairngorms before passing through the Feshie gorge into the Feshie valley. There is a small corrie above Achlean, part of a small tributary of the Feshie where deer herds sometimes gather. Many years ago this part was named Ciste Mhearad, Margaret's Coffin, but legends differ as to Margaret's identity. One tells of a Margaret who, jilted by the Mackintosh of Moy of that time, wandered aimlessly in the glen until she died. Another story has it that Mackintosh of Moy condemned a young man to death and that Margaret, the convicted man's sweetheart, begged for mercy but to no avail. She put a curse on Mackintosh and his family, which threatened that the chiefship should never more descend from father to son. Her body was found in Ciste Mhearad.

Another tradition recalls the haunting of the corrie by a 'wretched hag', who, having been driven out of her village because of the crimes she had committed, looked after her goats there until she eventually found her own grave. Yet another tale does not mention any crimes or atrocities carried out by the Margaret who herded goats, but relates that, in the course of tending her flock in the corrie, she searched for Cairngorm crystals and had her own 'ciste', or 'chest', in the corrie where she hid her findings. In the old days Ciste Mhearad was known to be covered in snow throughout the year, but this is no longer so in our changing climate.

Sir Edwin Landseer used to spend his holidays in this area, becoming inspired to paint many of his famous works of art, notably *The Monarch of the Glen*. He decorated the interior walls of mountain bothies in which he stayed with drawings of animals' heads, much to the delight of other visitors.

Although Glenfeshie was an ideal location for an airfield, there were some initial drawbacks that had to be resolved. In all, the strip was approximately 1,000 yards long, but about 200 yards down it was traversed by a fence on the edge of a deep ravine. The club members had many ideas about possible ways of dealing with this obstacle. At first the club launched their gliders straight over it, but after a few incidents they started to fill it in with rocks, old cars and junk. Quite a lot of the material was spoil generated by the building of the new A9, including timber debris dumped there, but ultimately Jane Williamson and her brother brought in a digger to complete the job. One old banger in particular, formerly owned by Sandy Lindsay and latterly used for towing gliders, had originally belonged to the late Queen Mother at Balmoral. The car, a Ford V8 Pilot, registered TLP4, was apparently first bought from Balmoral by Sandy through a dealer. He then sold it on to a pathologist who lived in Badenoch and wanted it for his children to play in! Before this operation was complete, the gliders had to be lifted by a winch, taking off at the other end of the field, which enabled them to clear the fence. The field was eventually improved when a grant of £5,000 was secured for the purpose of levelling and re-seeding the ground.

Bill Longstaff well remembered the first winch, a converted former army vehicle which the members bought from a gliding club near Kinross. They could not afford a two-seater glider to begin with and had to make do with a single-seater. Apparently it was quite common in those days to learn to fly while being pulled along the ground in a ground-slide, which enabled student pilots to work the controls and keep the wings level, after which they would be instructed on how to keep a correct gliding angle in pitch. Each wing of the modified training glider was fitted with big vertical boards, which were supposed to prevent the glider from taking off. 'They would make little hops up and back, nothing too dangerous,' Bill told me, 'and then it was up for your first solo flight.' However, though the training machine was heavily weighted, there came a notable day when another of the founder members, Angus McLeod, amazed everyone when he took off in it and climbed to about 20 or 30 feet. In theory this should not have happened; the next thing was that they saw him drop almost straight down. Luckily nothing but his pride was injured, but the glider was a write-off. This gave the members the impetus and legitimate reason to buy a two-seater!

There was no hangar to begin with, so when two gliders were purchased for the club, they were stored for the winter in Kingussie at the Duke of Gordon Hotel, which was owned and managed by Bill and Gillian Paterson, also founder members. Fortunately for the gliding club, the hotel used to be closed at that time of year because it was so difficult to heat. Even though, as Bill wryly observed, it was like Colditz inside, repairs were being made on the older glider, using scraps of metal and old tablecloths.

Bill assured me that on the whole gliders were very safe. The few accidents that had occurred were minor. Once or twice there had been landings in rivers, even on Loch Morlich when it was frozen solid, or gliders had landed on top of trees, but normally it was only the glider that was damaged. However, on one occasion when a lady pilot went up in a single-seater glider, a pregnant ewe got caught up in the cable. The unfortunate animal was lifted about 300 feet before it dropped and splattered on the ground below. The insurer headed his letters, 'Prime Ewe, Deceased'.

Bill Macdonald described the excitement as the original members gradually realised their dream of having their own gliding club in Badenoch and Strathspey. As if it were yesterday, he remembered the steps taken to establish the club as a going concern. They bought an old bus from Smithy, who owned Smith's Garage, and once they had taken out the seats and the whole back panel, two de-rigged gliders could fit into the space. 'This was our first building, so to speak,' he said. Later, Jane bought for the club a Nissen hut in which several gliders, fully rigged for flight, could easily be stored. Unfortunately, not long after that, the hut was damaged by a tornado and had to be rebuilt, somewhat smaller, out of the remains that were salvageable. At a later date a similar tornado completely destroyed another glider, which had been left in a trailer outside the hut. Even though the aircraft was thrown 12 feet into the air, then bounced lightly on one corner and finally landed in pieces in the river, the hangar remained intact. It still exists and is used to store trailers during the winter.

As I sat in front of the fire at Blackmill Farm talking to Bill and May Macdonald, we could hear the tugs at work, pulling gliders up into the peaceful skies. This reminded Bill of a story, which he then related: 'My friend Peter Forbes, who had a business in Perth for some time, landed a Cessna about 150 yards from here. He was also a flying instructor in Aberdeen and had been gliding on this occasion. He was always looking for a challenge.' Bill paused as he listened to an aircraft above and then continued. 'One day he told me that he was going skiing in the Cairngorms the following morning, and that in the afternoon he would come back and that we would go flying together.'

Bill smiled as he remembered the rest of the story. He had waited and waited. Peter never came, so after stopping for lunch, Bill carried on working as usual. Much later in the day Bill found out that Peter had come back late but could not find him, and so had taken the Cessna up on his own. Peter had been skiing on Cairngorm that morning and at the top had found the snow was frozen rock-hard underfoot. He had even jumped up and down on the ice to test it. What fun it would be to land the aeroplane on top of the solid snow, he had thought. So back he had come, returning to the summit in his Cessna. What he had forgotten about was the afternoon sun and its effect on the ice. The ice had melted and, as he landed, his front wheel caught in the slush, causing the aircraft to flip over onto its back. His subsequent embarrassment was further compounded by having to dismantle the whole plane in order to get it down the slopes. Fergus Williamson lent him his farm lorry to transport it back to Edinburgh for repairs.

Blackmill Farm is hidden in a little hollow off the road to the airstrip, near an outdoor activity centre called Lagganlia. Before the latter was built there were only a few cottages dotted around, but there was a good village spirit about the place. 'In the old days,' Bill said, 'the houses were counted by the "smokes", these being the chimneys.' The local folk watched for the smoke coming out of their neighbours' chimneys, and that is how they knew all was well. No smoke and there would be enough concern to instigate a visit. 'Our elderly neighbour would always look out for her brother, who lived in the cottage across the way. One morning she said to me that she had seen his smoke in the morning, but that there was no smoke at all by the afternoon. I immediately went over and indeed, it was bad news. I found him outside, between the old privy and the house. He had had a heart attack.'

We talked away the morning and the heat of the day, along with the sound of aeroplanes, made the thought of going up into the blue skies in a glider more and more enticing. I had only once been up in one, when the children were very young, but I had never intended to repeat this performance. However, having just heard the stories told with such passion, I wondered whether to forget my misgivings.

'Is it really safe?' I asked Bill. 'Do you think I should try again?'

'You'll never get a more perfect day,' he replied. 'The skies are blue, a clear day and there's just enough wind to be good, but gentle.'

It was now or never, before I changed my mind. The weather was indeed perfect, unusually hot for March, and the roof of my car was down as I drove towards the airstrip. I felt excited, but also nervous. Before going to see Bill and May I had stopped off at the airfield and spoken at length with some of the club members who had, like Bill, encouraged me to return for a flight. So here I was: I had returned and they were very welcoming. I was told to drive to the bottom of the airstrip, to the green caravan. I did not know the depth of the potholes, which were filled with water, so I drove with exceeding care, avoiding those I could, but driving even more slowly through those I couldn't. It took a while to reach the other end.

A single-seater glider was tied to the tug-plane and was about to take off. I watched as it was pulled with ease into the air, gently following its leader and disappearing behind the only cloud in the sky. When it reappeared on the other side, much smaller but still attached, I saw it soar higher and higher, then make for the hills before being let loose to fly alone. Then it was gone.

This was my opportunity to talk to club members and also to a couple of first-time recruits. Of the two younger members there that day, one still attended Kingussie High School and the other was a student at Caledonian University in Glasgow. It was his father who had just taken off in the single-seater. Anyone who is prepared to wait for hours a day just to go up for about half an hour must be keen, I thought. Don Grant from Invergordon told me how he had first become interested in planes. He was given a flight in an aeroplane for Christmas one year and had enjoyed it so much that he longed to take up flying, but gliding, he thought, would be a cheaper option. He heard of a gliding website, looked through it and found the Feshie club, of which he had now been a staunch member for four years. What a contrast to his job as a cooper in a whisky distillery! He told me that making barrels for whisky kept him inside, whereas gliders took him out, and that he found being up in the sky in a glider both terrifying and exhilarating. 'Beautiful to see the mountains from a height, and being really high you can relax, knowing that you are not going to hit the ground.' He spoke with the ardour he clearly felt for this sport, as did everyone else I spoke to that day.

While I was hanging around waiting my turn, I spoke to a young man who had just been up in the air. Though from Clydebank, he was currently working nearby at the Lagganlia centre. He told me that his flight had been fantastic, but admitted that he had been quite nervous beforehand. What brought potential danger into his mind was the fact that, while he was still on the ground and being assisted with his parachute, his instructor had said, 'In the unlikely event . . . but no one has ever had to use one!' Having heard this, I have to say that in anticipation of my own flight, I too began to worry! I also wondered why the tug-plane had stopped minutes before taking off, for although the rope was attached and both were ready to go, both had come to a halt. What would happen if he stalled in the air, glider in tow? I was becoming increasingly edgy, but should not have doubted the tug-pilot's expertise. The wind had changed direction, as it continued to do all afternoon, and so the flight was delayed until the wind was favourable. I began to doubt whether I would ever have a chance to go up myself, but my turn finally came.

I was harnessed into my parachute by Don, who was very professional, telling me which straps I should bring around my inner legs and secure to the front. I managed with no problems, but the parachute felt very heavy. I then had the task of getting into the glider with this weight on my back; having been firmly told not to touch the canopy, I lunged with difficulty into the plane and found myself lying backwards. I was almost settled, bracing myself for this new experience, only to be told to get out. The wind had changed and we were to launch the glider from the other side of the airstrip. I staggered out like the Michelin Man, weighted and ungainly. Off came the parachute and I was back to square one, helping to manoeuvre the aircraft.

'Hold the wing up as we take it around,' commanded Don. 'I didn't know we had to run,' I said as we set off across the field. 'If I had known I would have been doing this, I would have had the appropriate footwear, not high-heeled boots!' The glider was swivelled around and then attached to a vehicle, after which effort I got back in my car and circumnavigated the pot-holes once more.

Having arrived at the other end of the airstrip, I waited again for my turn to go up in the glider. Once it had been pulled towards us, we had to position ourselves, one to head, one to wing (me), and we were off running again. The next performance was to put the parachute on and I was very pleased with myself, remembering the instructions. Back into the glider and down I went into the seat at great speed, the weight of the parachute tilting me backwards and depositing me low into the seat.

We then came across another hurdle before take-off. I was too light for the aircraft, which meant weights had to be added beneath my left leg, but these were in the green caravan at the other side of the airstrip, so one of the young men was given the task of returning over the pot-holes to fetch them. In the meantime, Don gave me instructions on the instruments in the cockpit. I felt vulnerable being in the front seat, even though before getting into the glider with my parachute, I had heard the previous instructions, 'In the unlikely event that you are told to get out etc.', and had been told how and when to open my parachute. 'No one has ever had to use one', was again quickly added.

The weights were duly placed below my left leg, which had to be strategically raised across to the right side of the cockpit to allow them to be secured. Don was impressed with my agility! It was usually an exceedingly difficult process, I was told. 'The weights will not shift whilst in flight?' I asked, worried in case they were left in mid-air when we dropped – a stupid remark considering the laws of gravity, but made in apprehension. I was assured that the weights were solid and fixed.

The wind was in the right direction, a little more gusty than before, and the deep blue of the sky was interrupted only by a few fluffy clouds. Bob Forrest, my pilot, carefully went through every necessary instruction. The tug came across and we were attached. As we were pulled along, I asked Bob if we were safe. 'Put it this way,' he laughed, 'I have a family waiting for me at home and I intend to go back to them tonight.' That was good enough for me!

By now we were soaring up into the sky. It was both frightening and exhilarating. 'What do I hold on to?' I asked, desperately wanting to clutch on to something, but finding nothing. 'Hold on to your harness straps if you must hold on to something,' I was told, 'but you don't need to hold on to anything. Just relax.' Relax! I was nevously anticipating the jolt and the drop.

Following release from the aerotow, the glider pulled up to the left, enabling its pilot to see that the glider had successfully released itself and was free. I need not have worried about the thump and sudden drop, which I was forewarned about, for unsurpassed peace followed; no engine, no noise. The total silence and tranquillity took my breath away: I felt like a bird.

The rock-face neared, as I had been primed, but I had not expected to see it in such proximity. All I could see was sheer rock in front of me as we gently swooped in to catch the hill lift. This, as had been explained to me before take-off, was a current of air that would aid our ascent. An up-draught hits the hill, rising up its side, enabling the glider to be manoeuvred into the rising air so that it can soar above the hill. Two other varieties of lift are described as thermal and waves, the latter being associated with long, cigar-shaped clouds. It seemed to take two or three hill-shots into the rock-face before we took off across the valley.

'The ground will suddenly drop from underneath you,' Bob told me just before I noted the sheer drop. There was so much space below us and tiny images which quickly became recognisable, albeit minute, as we soared downwards. I could see little houses and the river curving gracefully through its valley like a nonchalant serpent passing time. Gradually I relaxed my grip on the harness and took in these tremendous views, which I had never seen at such an angle before. All looked so green, so vast, yet so small. Below spread evergreens and pine woods across from Rothiemurchus to Glenmore, and the gleaming surfaces of Loch Insh and the 'Second Loch Insh', as Bob described the winter floods where waters over the marshes and rivers mingled. I could see how gliding could become an addictive pastime.

This airfield, which provides many with such excitement and pleasure, has been well-established over the years and there are enthusiastic members from all over the country: there must be very few gliding clubs with such scenery. The founder members certainly found a perfect spot for an airstrip in Badenoch and Strathspey. Even I, terrified as I am of heights, was so exhilarated on that 'perfect day for gliding', making trips into the thermals and hill-lifts, that I simply had to take out a provisional membership!

8

Loch Insh

LOCH INSH (meaning 'island' or 'water meadow') was named after a hillock called Tom Euanan, which often became an island in times of flooding. In the middle of the hillock is a little church dating from the seventh century, called either St Euanan or Adamnan, after St Columba's biographer, who was said to have spent many days there. He warned the local people that if his cast-iron handbell was ever taken out of the church, it would make its own way back to where it rightly belonged. When it was stolen one day, some believed that it had been taken as far as Edinburgh, whereas others thought it had been removed to cure a sick man at St John's in Perth. The bell miraculously became free and made its own way home across the hills and up over Drumochter, where it rang out, 'Tom Euanan, Tom Euanan'. The ancient church was first restored in the 1820s, but since then further improvements have been made over the years, and it is now kept in good repair by the Badenoch Christian Centre.

Not far from Loch Insh, between Kingussie and Kincraig, are the Insh Marshes, which are subject to flooding, especially when the Spey is in spate or there has been a thaw. Nevertheless, the whole area draws visitors, particularly because of the great diversity of wild flowers, as well as other plants and trees of interest, with the added attraction of the area being an RSPB reserve. Today, water-sports are offered on Loch Insh thanks to Clive and Sally Freshwater.

Clive, who came from Lincolnshire, had qualified as a teacher of physical education and also played professional football with Leeds United. In the early 1960s he injured his back while at college and was then unable to continue his football career. Sometime later he moved north to Glenmore Lodge, near Kingussie, where he was taken on as an instructor in outdoor activities and hillwalking. He was already a keen canoeist and had even made his own canoe, building the wooden frame in a scout hut in Mablethorpe; the gas he used for boiling the glue had come to 52 shillings, more than the wood had cost! One of his duties at Glenmore Lodge was to teach children Scottish country dancing and, not having done this before, he had to quickly learn all the steps from Jack Morrison, a well-known instructor from Glasgow.

Every year sixty boys came from Glasgow in October and sixty girls in November and they stayed the whole month. 'I cut my teeth teaching the boys,' Clive told me. He knew what kind of behaviour to expect from the children. Some of them came from rough schools and there were always problems, such as Coke bottles being thrown down the corridor until they smashed at the bottom. 'If their behaviour was atrocious, we could make their lives pretty miserable: they would be put "ben the hoose", as it was called,' said Clive, explaining that meant they were confined to a stone-flagged corridor with no heating. If the boys were absolutely outrageous, they had to sleep in their sleeping-bags on that stone floor for the night. The children were taken all over the Cairngorms and enjoyed many different sports, probably for the first time in their lives. Although their behaviour could be impossible to begin with, they usually conformed by the time they were halfway through their stay there and when the month was over, many of those unruly boys were in tears as they said their goodbyes.

'We even took the children snow-holing in the winter,' Clive recalled. He would never forget one particular night in November when he took a party of schoolgirls camping about three miles from Glenmore Lodge. Clive was in the Ryvoan Bothy and the girls were in tents, three of them in each, lying only on ground-sheets. Throughout the night there was a heavy fall of snow, amounting to over two feet, and the tents collapsed. Unfortunately, because there were no radios or phones, they had to cope by themselves. Although a tall man, even Clive was thigh-deep in the snow, which took half the day to clear before they could pack up and go home.

Many years previously, when the old lodge at Glenmore was still a youth hostel and the new training centre had yet to be completed, the warden at that time had a strange encounter. It was mid-afternoon when he noticed a female student and her instructor return to the lodge. They came into the main hall and walked through to the common room and the warden, thinking that it was too early for them to return, presumed that the pupil was either exhausted or had developed blisters, which often happened if the footwear was unsuitable. Later that afternoon, however, the police arrived at the door to inform the warden that the instructor and student had been killed in a corrie. The warden gathered that the accident had happened earlier that day, before his experience, which both saddened and mystified him.

The first warden of the new lodge, who was in charge for many years, also had a story about a bizarre incident there, which occurred one night when it was snowing heavily. He heard raucous voices coming from outside and, looking out of the window, saw lights amongst the trees. When he went out to investigate, he found no sign of anyone there at all, nor indeed that anyone had been there, for there were no footprints in the snow. No one ever discovered an explanation for this disturbance.

There is also a legend about the spectre of the Bodach Lamh Dhearg (the spectre of the bloody hand, or Red-Handed Carl), which was reputed to appear in the vicinity of Glenmore. Robin Og Stewart of Kincardine was once gralloching [removing the entrails of] a stag in those parts when the Bodach Lamh Dhearg appeared at his side. It was believed that the ghostly being, known to be the protector of the local deer, lived at the east side of the sands of Loch Morlich and that it brought a warning of some kind to those to whom it manifested itself. The sudden apparition of the Bodach Lamh Dhearg filled Robin with horror and he noticed blood dripping from one of its hands. The spectre admonished and threatened him, and told him to go away immediately. So intimidated did he feel that day that he never hunted in the region again. The fearsome spectre was said to have been in fact a kindly old gentleman who only tormented with dire threats those who hurt the creatures he tried to shield. Another tradition indicated that he was actually a fairy knight disguised as a fierce warrior, which explained the bloody hand!

***

Clive Freshwater had many hidden talents. He was a folk singer as well as an entertainer and in the 1960s, he and others formed the Wild Rover Folk Club at Carrbridge, where he would go from Glenmore in the evenings to sing and play his guitar at the hotel. Many of his songs were Glasgow street songs, with anti-polis or -royal words, which he learnt from the children who came to stay at the centre. He sang me snatches of some of them in his fine voice, which I thoroughly enjoyed. He also told me an amusing story about his days as an entertainer, which involved himself and his friend, Eric Beard, nicknamed 'Beardie', who held the record for climbing the Four Tops from Glenmore over Braeriach, Cairn Toul, Ben MacDui and Cairngorm and back in four and a half hours! Eric was another of the founding members of the folk club and so, when the Aviemore Centre was about to be opened, he and Clive decided to grasp an opportunity to raise money for their club. They approached the general manager of the centre and asked him if they could play at the opening. It was unfortunately too late to advertise, but the management agreed that they could play free of charge in the Osprey Room, where their event was due to take place. All the same, advertising of some sort was essential and so Beardie, with a billboard over his neck, went up the slopes to the top of the White Lady. He was wearing short mountaineering skis, and was dressed in blue and white striped pyjamas, ringing a bell as he shouted, 'There's a folk night tonight! There's a folk night tonight!' Because the skis were short, he ran like a duck. 'He was some spectacle,' Clive recalled, 'and everyone took note.' That night 550 people turned up, which amazed and shocked the manager. Clive and Beardie were thrilled to have 2s. 6d. per head. At least the hotel had the bar trade from the crowd, which was better than no takings at all. Back at the lodge, Beardie was so exhilarated that he threw the notes into the air and watched them float down to the floor. 'Those were Klondyke years,' Clive added.

Eager to start his own water-sports business, Clive tried to secure a lease at both Loch-an-Eilan and Loch Alvie, but was unsuccessful. Then, after much negotiation, he finally got a year's lease at Loch Insh for the purpose. Even though the landowners, the Forestry Commission, were not supportive of his venture, a merchant banker, the fishing-tenant at the time, was delighted. 'Ah yes, sailing,' he said in response to Clive's phone call. 'We have a catamaran – but keep away from the fishing boats.' In the late 1960s as many as 100 salmon would be caught in Loch Insh annually, once they had swum up the River Spey from the sea, making fishing one of the most important activities in the area. Thus began a new business that later was named the Cairngorm Canoeing and Sailing School Ltd, which today trades as Loch Insh Water Sports.

When May Brown, one of the founders of Glenmore Lodge, heard that Clive intended to start up a water-sports company, she advised him not to leave his present job until the new venture was established. This, however, was not to be, for Clive had to leave because of some personal ill-feeling between himself and the management. After that, Clive went on the dole for three months and started to push forward his new venture as quickly as he could. It eventually opened in a small way, with only a wooden shack on the beach, six canoes, one sailing-boat and one member of staff, a young university student as a beach girl. Luckily, during the first season, Insh village hall came up for sale and Clive managed to buy it so that he and his wife had somewhere to live until they had built up the business.

Their biggest setback was a writ served on them in 1972 by a company that owned certain stretches of the Spey. Clive's wife, Sally, had previously been intercepted while canoeing on the river and the ensuing writ accused them of disturbing the fishing. It was a shock, but Clive was determined to fight this attempt to prevent canoeing on the river to the bitter end. His lawyer felt that he probably had a 50/50 chance of winning his case, but that even if he managed to get hold of the local ghillies to discuss the fishing, many would probably be loyal to their employers, the estate owners. However, he knew half the ghillies, because they used to listen to him singing in the hotels and they at least stood by him. It was common knowledge that many fish were caught by anglers after canoes had gone through the pools, therefore it was not possible to condemn canoes as detrimental to fishing. Clive's QC researched the history of canoeing on Scottish rivers (it could be traced back to the 1920s) and found interesting information regarding floating timber, which had been found not to disturb the fishing. Clive had the pleasure of interviewing an elderly lady, in her youth a nurse in the Boer War, who told him that she clearly remembered going down to the river at Kingston-on-Spey to see the last of the floats by the schoolmaster's house in 1885. She was also cited by the other side in court, but being very deaf, she thought they were talking about the timber floats, not the fishing, so was no help to them at all.

The appeal, the final hearing of which lasted three weeks, was, until recently, the longest Scottish case ever heard in the House of Lords, the protracted account of which Clive hopes to write in his retirement. Interestingly enough, the obituary of Lord Maxwell, who chaired the proof (where the written statements are taken), noted that he had considered the 'Spey Case' the most important of all he had ever presided over. Though a keen fisherman himself, he had been very much in favour of the Freshwaters' side of the dispute.

9

Local Characters

ALL villages have their characters, often to be found in the local pub. The 'Wood 'n' Spoon' in Kingussie used to be a wonderful meeting place, with its restaurant at one side and the bar, called The Creel, on the other. David and Kathy Russell ran it as a family business and have many good stories about their time there. One particular local worthy called Jock, a gamekeeper, lived in a caravan on the Insh road near Torcroy. 'He was sort of a sad case,' Kathy told me. 'You would see him riding his bicycle with three or four rabbits over his shoulders and more hanging from the handle bars – and he was often taken for a ride,' she added. 'On a Thursday, after he collected his dole money, he would come into the pub and be persuaded to buy everyone a drink. He was amazing: I was told that if he put down twenty-five snares for rabbits, he would catch twenty-five rabbits.'

Kathy smiled when she spoke of Jock, who was a gamekeeper and the only person known to make the deer run towards him. 'The way he did this was to drive them into a cul-de-sac in the hills, fire a shot at the cliffs, which would ricochet, causing the frightened deer to turn away from the noise and run towards him.' David took over the story: 'Getting home for him was a nightmare, after a night in the pub. There would be nights when Jock would fall flat on his face, only to find himself in a ditch the next morning, and indeed he was once discovered covered in frost. Taxi drivers were wary of giving him a ride, knowing that he might be "ill" on the way home.' Jock would be heard to say, as he staggered out of the pub. 'I know where I'm going, Choo Choo Baby,' which was what he tended to call everybody.

David gave him a lift one night, but as they went under the bridge near Ruthven, Jock was adamant that he was being taken home the wrong way. The bridge was new and Jock had completely forgotten about it. He kept insisting that they were on the wrong road, until David was eventually forced to give in to him and had to turn back to see if he could find anyone who knew the supposedly correct route. The only person around at 2 a.m. was the signal man at the railway station, so David climbed up into the signal box to ask the way to Jock's caravan. 'Under the bridge and straight on up the hill,' he was told, just as he had believed in the first place!

'OK, home! Can we get in?' David asked when they finally arrived at Jock's caravan.

'No problem, Choo Choo Baby. The key's on the tree.'

'Which tree?' David asked, looking at the forest that sheltered the caravan.

'The tree I always keep it in,' was the answer.

Even in the beam of the car's headlights, no key was found on any tree, and by this time Jock had fallen flat on his face in the snow. There was no alternative: David had to try to get into the caravan without a key. He climbed on top of the bonnet of the car, stretched up to reach a small window which looked down onto an old cooker inside Jock's home and opened it without much difficulty. Leaping through, he tried hard to miss pots full of bones in putrefying stock and disgusting dog food as he fell to the floor. The smell was quite appalling, but was made even worse when he knocked over a couple of pans of these vile mixtures. Obliged to hold his breath, he bolted straight out of the door, and then dragged Jock inside for the night and left him oblivious to the mess around him. Jock was a hardy man and survived many life-threatening incidents that others might not, but he was well-liked in the villages and there always seemed to be a hand to help him in times of need.

Wherever there is shooting or fishing, poaching has always been fairly predictable, even today. Poachers of old were characters, often respected for their skills, considered as Robin Hoods who took for the pot rather than the purse, though if the catch was too large, selling it was a better option. Victor Stockwell was a likeable chap who one evening walked into The Creel absolutely soaking wet, as Kathy said. He asked to see the Russells, who found him dripping, wearing a bold, toothy grin. He stood there, proudly holding a salmon of about 25lb, a considerable catch for a day's work. He had caught it at the Falls of Truim on Glentruim Estate. With great pride, and no sense of shame, Victor began to tell of his day's poaching. Everyone in the bar craned their necks to hear, riveted by the tale that unfolded. He was a clever poacher and the locals loved to hear about Victor's daring ploys.

During this long day, Victor had been at the bottom of the falls, well aware that he should not have been there in the first place, forever watchful lest the water bailiffs should be on patrol and spot him. Suddenly he got a bite and there, at the end of his line, was a mammoth fish jumping and splashing in the water. Tinged by the fading light, the salmon sparkled as it pulled and writhed while gradually being reeled in. Playing his fish, he heard a sound and wondered if it could have been a foot on a twig, a shifting stone or perhaps an animal of the night. Listening and watching cautiously, he gave the fish some slack to allow free movement, so that it would not thrash about, thus rousing attention. In a trice, the next thing that happened was that, having been given a long line, the salmon easily managed a gigantic leap upwards, reaching the top of the falls with great elegance. That left Victor holding the rod below, imagining the huge salmon smug in the pool above. Knowing that there could be someone around, Victor climbed the rocks at the side of the falls as quietly as he could. With every step he took, he wandered a little closer to the water's edge, watching the salmon but also keeping an eye on the banks for the spoiler of his sport. On reaching the top of the falls he began to wind the handle on his reel, until the line was fairly taut and when he was level with the fish, he released it a little until it slackened slightly. Suddenly, the next thing he knew, the reel was spinning and the fish had slithered successfully back down to the bottom pool! He scrambled back down the rocks at the edge as fast as he could, adrenaline flowing, primitive instinct driving him to his prey. In his fury at being outwitted by a fish, his fear of being caught poaching by the bailiff disappeared. Therefore, when he reached the bottom pool he jumped straight into the water with one aim in mind, forgetting his waders, which immediately filled with water and dragged him down. Hastily shaking off his gear, he managed to dive at the fish and coil his arms around it, but it slipped through, quick as lightning, hitting the surface of the water. In the meantime most of Victor's fishing equipment was lost, except for his rod, which he could see upstream. Dispirited, he waded chest-high in the freezing water and grabbed his rod, which to his astonishment still had the fish on the end of its line. His excitement gave him renewed energy and with little effort the exhausted salmon was landed. Victor was triumphant.

The pub-goers that night had a great story to take home, although the fish itself was far too big for Victor to take home for the pot. The only alternative was to sell it, which is why he had turned up at the bar. Kathy, who was nine months pregnant with her youngest son at the time, laughed so much when she heard this story that she went into labour. For obvious reasons, 15 May 1978 was always a significant date for David and Kathy thereafter.

Unfortunately Victor Stockwell was killed on his motor-bike as he went round a dangerous corner between Newtonmore and

Kingussie. This was a doubly sad part of the road for us, because our labrador was also run over and killed there. A vast number of people attended Victor's funeral, for he had many admirers. Though much missed, he will always be remembered, for he has left a legacy of tales in the village where he grew up.

Victor's widow, Eileen, chatted to me about her late husband and told me some of his achievements. 'He was good at everything he turned his hand to,' she said, proudly recounting his talents. 'He was a superb artist and I am sure there are pictures of his in many of the houses around here, in Newtonmore,' she added. She told me Victor had made fine cross-bows for sporting purposes, whereas his peers made ordinary bows. There was even a time when Victor made a very professional specimen of a silencer for a gun. Motor-bikes were another hobby of his and he enjoyed buying parts from antique and second-hand shops for the purpose of constructing his own models. Victor undertook various different lines of work in his time and seemed to master any of the trades that he engaged in, with great proficiency. While working for a butcher, he became accomplished in all aspects of skinning and butchering. He was also a good chef and could cook game to perfection.

As proved by his epic tussle with the salmon, Victor was an expert angler; he could tie his own flies and won most of the men's fly-casting competitions in the valley, while his wife won numerous ladies' events. However, fishing permits were not something Victor gave much thought to and Eileen loved to talk about his poaching expeditions. 'He would often go over Garva, past Loch Spey and get himself down to Roy,' she said, her smile hinting at the forthcoming tale of a 'Victor' prank. Then she added, 'He caught ponies on the way so that he could go for more salmon! The salmon were too heavy to carry, so he would sling them over the pony's back. On his return, when he reached his motor-bike, he would transfer the fish from pony to bike and when the pony's work was done, he would set it free.'

Ponies were traditionally used for bringing back deer from the hills, rather than fish from the rivers. Eileen recalled a time when Victor had walked for miles across the Monadhliaths to shoot a hind. 'Up the back, about ten miles over the hill, there was a croft,' Eileen told me, 'and there was always an old white pony in the field. It had been a very successful night: Victor had shot two stags and it must have been around four in the morning when he struggled homeward, dragging the beasts behind him. He was exhausted. It was tough enough to pull one, let alone two. Spotting the white pony, he grabbed it and slung one of the deer over its neck. As Victor was about to set off, dragging the other beast behind him, the pony bent her head round and gave him a sniff! Wondering whether she would take another, he slung the second deer over its back and waited for a few moments to see whether the mare would keep it. She did, so he led the pony carrying two red deer home to the bottom gate, behind the houses here.' Eileen was laughing as she pointed to the rear of the house, remembering the scenario. 'He slipped the deer off the pony and slapped it on its bum, then off it went, back up the hill towards home.'

Victor was certainly one of the charmed poachers, an individual with a striking personality, which made it difficult for local landlords to take serious action when he was caught out, especially if the catch was just for the pot.

The Creel bar had originally been a craft shop. Kathy and David, being extremely involved with the restaurant in their early years, employed a talented craftsman to run the shop for them. He was ideal for the job and proved able to turn his hand to anything. For instance, the Russells asked him to make a sign for the restaurant, any kind of sign; it was left up to him, as long as it would attract custom. After much thought an enormous wooden spoon was made, which was fixed above the door of the establishment. It was an eye-catching piece of

86

workmanship that one could not miss while driving through Kingussie.

A few weeks after the craftsman had made the magnificent wooden spoon, David gave him a lift home so that he could pick up a ladder he had asked to borrow. David's employee's home was rent-free in exchange for essential renovations he was carrying out. As soon as David walked into the hall of the house he could not help but notice a large hole in the floor-boards, cut out with a jig-saw in the shape of a spoon! Part of the front staircase was also missing and the children were reaching the first floor by stepping onto six-inch nails strategically inserted into the main staircase pillar. Access to the next two floors was by the ladder which David had come to borrow. The ladder had to be used for one more task before being taken away that night. It was placed against the wall by the electricity meter, which was reversed with a screwdriver, ready for the meter reader, who would have found their energy consumption low! David's employee had certainly turned out to be a very 'handy' man.

Further up the valley, Eddie Orbell was head-hunted in 1971 to organise the construction of the Highland Wildlife Park, which is situated between Kingussie and Aviemore. The plan was to form a living museum by establishing a collection of wildlife that had formerly been indigenous to the Highlands. Some creatures were brought in from local areas, others Eddie had to search for all over Britain and Europe.

We gave the wildlife park their first four wildcat kittens, from Glentruim. They had been deserted by their mother and one of our friends, who had been out shooting first thing in the morning, had found them, put them in a sack and brought them back to my kitchen. The kittens withdrew to a corner and were fierce, even at that early age; it was impossible to get close to them without being scratched to bits. Eddie came to collect them, after which they were hand-reared until old enough to feed themselves.

Where there are wild and dangerous animals, there are always tales to be told. Przewalskis, similar to the oldest breeds of European horse, are the only wild species left in existence and known to be very aggressive animals. When some of these were first purchased for the wildlife park, all visitors were warned not to get out of their cars or feed the animals, but these rules were often disregarded. In particular, there was one coach driver, Eddie told me, who enjoyed amusing his passengers by feeding apples to the horses while standing on the running-board of the coach. He did this so regularly that the horses had come to expect fruit each time they saw a coach. When other coaches came through and stopped with no offer of apples, the horses would then cross and viciously kick at the vehicles!

'There was also a roe buck,' Eddie reminisced. 'It had been hand-reared, but was very aggressive and not in the slightest frightened of humans. When one chap got out of his car to open his boot, the buck charged him, ramming him right up the backside and heaving him into the boot.' The tourist managed to get the beast by the horns, gripping tightly, and while he was being shaken up and down and right to left, his hair flying in one direction, then the other, Eddie went up to him and said, 'Well, you shouldn't be out of the car, should you?' The tourist had only himself to blame if he chose to ignore the many signs warning of danger.

On another occasion, a photographic competition had been advertised in the park and the father of a toddler came into Eddie's office with his snapshot. 'Could I submit this one?' The masterpiece was proudly held up for Eddie to examine: a picture of the tourist's little girl standing underneath a huge, ugly-looking bull bison, which was being offered a slice of bread from her tiny outstretched hand. Smiling broadly, the trusting infant was watching the dangerous creature as she waited for it to accept her morsel! She survived this potential disaster safely, with a winning photograph as proof of her luck, in more ways than one. Others might not have been so fortunate.

Glentruim House

Breakachy, Glentruim

Above. Cat Lodge

Right.
Eaun Macpherson of Glentruim

Loch Laggan from the air

Glider preparing for aero-tow

Eddie Orbell with bear cubs

Hill ponies; one carries a stag from Glenfeshie forest

Euan Macpherson of Glentruim on the hills of Glentruim

Ruthven Castle

John Allen in the Cairngorms

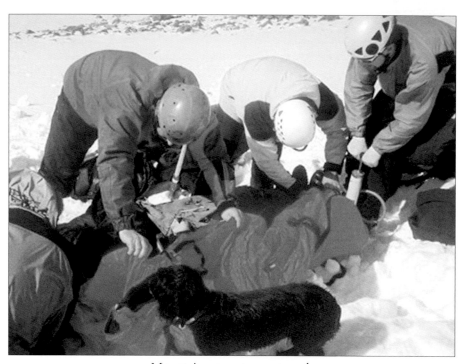

Mountain rescue team at work

Helicopter rescue in the Cairngorms

Shepherd on the hills with his collies

An illicit still

Above.
Back: Donald McCook,
far left, with guests.
Front: Mrs McCook,
Joseph McCook,
Elizabeth McCook

Left. Dr I.F. Grant

A 'blackhouse' at the Highland Folk Museum, Kingussie

Shinty on the Eilean, Newtonmore

Dancers at Highland Games of old on the Eilean

Right to left: Alastair Macpherson of Pitmain (clan chieftain),
Bill Macpherson of Cluny (clan chief), Euan Macpherson of Glentruim
(clan chieftain) and Jamie Macpherson, son of Cluny

Rob Ritchie lifting the Stone of Heroes at Newtonmore Games

Rob Ritchie throwing the 28-lb weight for distance

Various people offered their services to the wildlife park. Not all of them were able to be of much use, but Eddie told me about a fellow he had employed who loved all the creatures he came across so much that he would protect every one of them, even vermin. One day, as he was helping out by operating the Cairngorm chair-lift up by the Ptarmigan restaurant, he noticed a sparrow up ahead. Rather than risk hurting the bird, he brought the chair-lift to an abrupt emergency stop, leaving its passengers swinging furiously. His view was that all animals have the right to live; he would spring or break traps set by game-keepers, and would also destroy any mouse-traps he found. This man, who loved all the creatures in the wildlife park, taking an avid interest in their welfare, was certainly a dedicated and willing helper there.

Eddie particularly remembered an occasion when he was called out of the district to assist the recapture of a famous bear called Hercules, which had escaped from its owner, Andy Robin, while they were on Benbecula during a publicity campaign. Owner and bear had gone out swimming, but when Andy stopped, Hercules carried on, until he was out of sight. Three weeks later two crofters sighted the bear, and the rescue team was alerted.

After receiving the good news, Eddie and George Raffety, the local vet, were picked up by helicopter from the park and flown to South Uist in the hope of retrieving the fugitive. (The vet had to accompany the party by law, in order to load the dangerous tranquillizer drug into the dart.) Only after eight fruitless hours of searching did they come across the bear, which was hiding behind a rock in the very last place they looked. It swam around for a while before being chased back onto dry land by the helicopter. Eddie fired a tranquillising dart, but the strength of the down-draught from the rotor blades caused him to miss his target. The second shot was successful and so they made their descent. Eddie chased after the bear on foot and lassooed his neck, but unfortunately the anaesthetic had not been powerful enough to immobilise him. The men were pulled along untill they managed to creep up the rope, hand over hand, gradually getting close enough to administer a further dose by syringe. This had the desired effect, but Hercules unfortunately collapsed into a peat-hag [holes from which peat has been cut], thus prolonging the rescue somewhat. Eventually he was hauled out and wrapped in a large net, which Eddie managed to fix onto a hook on the undercarriage of the helicopter as it hovered overheard. Thus was the unconscious creature lifted and transported back to Benbecular before being delivered into the safe hands of his owners. In the meantime, poor Eddie was tormented by swarms of midges as he awaited the return of the helicopter to take him back to the Wildlfe park.

Eddie was also asked to deal with the Revack Black Cat, a feral cat trapped by a gamekeeper, which was thought to be the first cross between the wild and domestic strains. The cat had distinctive white guard-hairs, a short tail and long body, but has since died and is now on show, stuffed, in an Edinburgh museum. The other notable exercise concerning large cats in which Eddie was involved occurred in the early 1980s, when there was widespread publicity regarding the Cannich puma. Eddie had to collect it from a local farmer, who had allegedly managed to capture the animal. Strangely enough, it was quite tame and walked straight from the trap into a box placed alongside. After its death a taxidermist preserved its body, and it can be seen in the Inverness Museum. An old lady from the area where the puma was found refused to believe that such cats could be indigenous, telling everyone, 'I see these big cats regularly. They are dropped by Russian planes and come down by parachute!' Weird things can happen in the Highlands, but I cannot help feeling that this might be a little far-fetched!

The Highland Wildlife Park, which was opened to visitors in 1972, has proved popular, and is of great benefit to the region. The creatures there, though captive, are free to roam in their accustomed terrain, surrounded by trees and hills. It has expanded over the years, and is now owned by Edinburgh Zoo.

10

The Hills

THE Highlands stretch from estate to estate between little villages. Full-time resident landowners are in a minority, but what is constant is the presence of good, loyal gamekeepers and their families. They are often the ones that 'keep' the estates together, and thriving because of their vigilant gamekeepering.

Keepers tend to rely on each other. There seems to be a mutual understanding, a strong kindred spirit between them, which means that a colleague from a neighbouring estate is always prepared to give advice or assistance. Whether stalking, rough-shooting, trapping or going round fox dens, a fellow-keeper will oblige, should help be required. Stories of the hills, wildlife and hunting are locked in the memories of most keepers, but a few, however, have documented their days on simple notepads and put them away for others to find years after they have gone.

The late Angie Bain was a quiet, reserved man of great dignity, whom we were privileged to have working for us as keeper at Glentruim for many years. He was a professional in his line of work, very much of the old school and highly respected in the area. Angie, whose father had also been a gamekeeper, was born near the south shore of Loch Ericht, where the estate lodge and stalkers' cottages were extremely isolated, the only approach being across the water in a rowing-boat. This was near the land which old Kennedy called 'a terrible place', but where he had nevertheless lived for forty-five years! When Angie was six years old his family moved to the village of Newtonmore, a more populated area, easily accessible from the old A9.

He committed his memories to paper, in a little blue book, his longhand writings expressing his fervour for the hills. 'At a very early age I was attracted to the hills. First as a beater on the moors, but at the age of eleven, as a dog-boy at Glen Banchor.' His duties as dog-boy included such tasks as cleaning out kennels or getting dogs paired up in preparation for shooting expeditions. On the actual days of the shoots, he and the other boys had to stay behind with the ghillie and the pannier pony, but were expected to have fresh dogs ready if needed. Being so young, Angie often found the dogs were stronger than himself, but being also determined, he never gave up. 'Sometimes the eager dogs got the better of me and I lost my balance. They just dragged me along. I never let them go, however much they pulled.'

The dreaded midges, for which we are all prepared in Scotland, are mentioned in Angie's memoirs as being 'almost unbearable', at times millions of them descending on him and the dogs in his charge. During these moments of onslaught, the pony man was spared because of the smoke from the 'black twist' in the pipe he was drawing on, which kept the midges away, but others suffered from these ferocious beasties, their attack being one of the least pleasant events of the day.

Good days outweighed bad on the moors, but there could be wet seasons when the birds became very wild, not sitting on the ground for the dogs to seek out. This meant that the birds would be driven early in the season, which suited Angie very well, giving him much more time later in the year to check his beloved hills.

Long before Angie lived at Glenbanchor on the outskirts of Newtonmore, there were several crofts and hamlets scattered in this region, along the River Calder. Planted beside each croft would be a rowan tree, as they are superstitiously believed to ensure good luck and keep witches at bay. Behind the villages there were summer sheilings, where cattle were herded during the day for grazing, then taken back at night. Many householders would own a cow not only for its milk, but also so that they could make their own butter and cheese.

Living near the hills meant close contact with nature and the creatures of the land; there was no boredom for a country lad. One day, as Angie was playing shinty in a field by the road through Glenbanchor, he heard a pony approaching and when he turned to look, he saw a stag swaying gently to and fro from the saddle of his father's horse. Running first to the house to collect his father's skinning knife, he then made his way to the game larder to find out whether he could be of assistance. None was required, but this was his first lesson in the art of dealing with deer. Little did he know then that he was to use his father's knife to gralloch and skin innumerable animals in the future.

It was not surprising that Angie and other keepers of his generation were so skilled in their jobs, for many, like himself, would leave school at the age of fourteen to seek full-time employment on the hill. Angie wrote about the vast numbers of hares around when he first started work, and the memorable drives he had experienced. Looking back on his hunting days, there was a particularly exciting encounter he had documented concerning his first contact with a Monadhliath fox. He had been sent out during a snowstorm to see how many hares had come down from the top of the hills. He was excited, feeling very responsible and grown-up, because he was allowed to carry his own gun, which had belonged to his father, a very good hammer gun with Damascus steel barrels, full and half choke.

Up to the top of Glenbanchor Angie strode, and reached a point where he could sit to spy across the moor and into the distance. Before long he spotted a vixen making her way further up towards the highest point. Being young and athletic, he wasted no time, nimbly covering the gap between them. Halting on the top ridge, he gradually moved forwards until the fox came in sight. She was lying down on a mound, about 100 yards away, basking in the sun. Making a stealthy approach in full view, he took off his puttees and boots, gently easing his stocking-clad feet into the hard-packed snow, for he did not want to make a sound. Very gradually he got nearer and nearer to shooting distance, until from about sixty-five yards he gave her two barrels and bowled her over. By this time his feet were extremely cold and wet, but this did not deter him from feeling exhilarated by his achievement, as he slung the fox and boots over his shoulder and headed for home. The following day, in the absence of the fox, over 200 hares were shot on the hill.

During his time of keepering, Angie witnessed the very rare sight of a grouse migration. At the time, the owners of the estate had made a request for haunches of venison and so an experienced stalker and the young Angie set out for the hills in search of a hind, on a calm but not particularly cold morning. There was thick snow on the ground and it continued to fall heavily throughout the day. To begin with there was no sign of life at all, then suddenly, around a crag, hinds were seen above and to the left of the top ridge. Angie's companion fired an excellent shot and a hind dropped immediately.

While they were gralloching the deer in the deep snow, grouse appeared from the east, flying low. Angie noted that 'there were thousands of them strung out for miles, heading west. As the leading birds passed over the boundary between Glenbanchor and Cluny, they headed in a southerly direction.' It was presumed that they were heading for the Pass of Drumochter, to reach the lower hills of Perthshire beyond. The sight of a vast number of grouse, their wings all drumming together, was never to be forgotten by either man. The heavy fall of snow and lack of food was undoubtedly the reason for the grouse migration, according to Angie, and for many years after this extraordinary event, these birds were scarce throughout the valley. Angie added, in the last paragraph of his notes, 'It has been a source of wonder to me how a migration begins. Who are their leaders? There must be some strong urge to move, and as with wild geese, a sense of direction and destination.'

Hunters rely on their stalker or gamekeeper to take them to their beast on the hill, and on the whole their chances of a shot are good. A stroke of luck never goes amiss, however, and it has even been known to send good beasts right to one's doorstep which, although saving an exhausting trek, is not a particularly sporting way to achieve a 'head'. Tony, the husband of one of my best friends, reminded me of an occasion when Angie took him stalking for hinds on Glentruim. They walked several miles to the furthermost point of the estate, but saw no deer before they reached the march, where Glentruim land bordered the neighbouring estate, and then there was only one of any significance. A clean shot was taken, after which the hind had to be dragged for many miles to the road at the bottom of Glentruim Hills, as this was where they had left the Land Rover. Angie had a limp in those days, for in his youth one of his legs had been damaged when he was gored by a cow defending her calf. This never impeded his performance as a gamekeeper and he could walk for miles, just as he did that day with Tony.

On the way back, near our home farm, the men looked down towards the lower part of the valley and noticed about fifty hinds. There seemed to be a breakaway group running from the main herd towards the bottom fields at Glentruim, so out of interest, Tony and Angie left the vehicle outside the game larder and walked down to the walled garden. Just as they had expected, there, in between the fruit bushes, was the splinter herd of deer! Exhausted after the long trail home, Tony admitted, 'It was galling to think that what you had been looking for all day was at the bottom of the garden on your return!'

Bill Dey, now retired, was also a keeper all his life, as were his forebears. His children, including his daughter, became keepers and his wife's family were keepers too. One can certainly say that 'keepering' runs in the family!

Bill told me a story about Angie and Paul Sherlock (Paul is also sadly deceased). Paul had been shooting in the area and the two men had gone over to Dulnain for stalking, and had successfully shot a stag. They duly slung the deer over the saddle of their pony and were halfway up Goat's Burn when the mare collapsed. The beast would not get up: 'It just put its head down as if it were dying,' Bill heard later. The stalkers set off home for help, mortified by the fact that they had been defeated by a pony. In the meantime the stag was left lying on the ground by the burn.

Angie phoned Bill and told him there had been a disaster on the hill. 'A shooting accident,' was Bill's immediate thought, before Angie told him it was all to do with a pony. Bill was relieved but curious. The mare that had been carrying the beast down from the hill was having a heart attack, he was told, and it was surely dying. When questioned Angie reiterated, 'It would not lift its head; it is definitely dying.'

'Are you sure it is not playing up?' Bill enquired.

'No,' insisted Angie, 'the beast is dying.'

Paul phoned Bill later with the same story. There was no question of what had to be done. Bill told the two men that he would deal with the matter and that Barry Fairweather, the vet, should be summoned. Paul described exactly where the pony was to be found at Goat's Burn and suggested that they should all meet there early the next morning.

At first light Bill and Barry drove off in the Land Rover, to bring back the dead pony. The vehicle had to be left halfway up the hill and, as Bill said, 'It was lashing stair-rods, inky black dark. We ventured over peat-hags and heather, the roughest of ground, eventually arriving at the spot where the deer had been dumped. Barry staggered down, bag in hand, soaking wet.' There was no dead pony!

Paul arrived a short time after them and was immediately quizzed by the vet. 'Where's your dead pony, man?' There was no dead mare to be seen anywhere! 'You mean to say, you have brought us all this bloody way and no pony?' Together they all walked upstream and suddenly there was the mare, happily grazing a few yards away. Pointing in the direction of the animal, Barry shouted, 'There's your dead pony, Paul!' Barry was soaked to the skin, but the pony was alive and Barry was determined to get his 'pennyworth'. He filled a syringe and gave the poor unsuspecting animal a jag; after all, he had not suffered this journey for nothing. Bill never did discover what was in the syringe! The stag was flung over the pony, which was given a slap on the buttocks with a command of 'Off you go!' and off it went, fresh as could be, oblivious to the trouble its moment of rest had caused that previous night.

There could be many amusing incidents during a stalk, some of which were not so funny to their victims. One time a lady stalker went up the hill with the keeper Jock Kirkpatrick, looking for stags. They took with them a frisky pony, which would not stand still for an instant. Having successfully shot a beast, they loaded it onto the pony, which went round and round, its hooves digging into the soft ground, causing peat to fly all over the place.

'Jock got a dollop of peat in the face,' said Bill, recalling the story. 'He started to brush it away and out came an eye.'

'Me e'e, me e'e,' Jock was gasping, as the lady looked on in horror, thinking that the peat had poked out his eye. Jock got out his hanky and gave it a dicht (wipe), then put the glass eye back in again.' Apparently that story went round the district in a jiffy!

***

In the quiet, peaceful valley of Badenoch and Strathspey, one would never expect to hear of a kidnapping. However, in the 1970s just such an incident occurred. It did not take place in the area, but involved the owner of the Pitmain estate, where Bill Dey worked. The estate owner, a baron and a wealthy man, lived in Belguim and one horrendous day he was taken at gunpoint from his home town and kidnapped. The kidnapper had everything planned, having even prepared a mini-van ready for his hostage, filling it with food and essential equipment, which included a pair of handcuffs. When the baron was abducted, there was a struggle. He fought courageously and somehow managed to get on top of his assailant, who unfortunately shoved his pistol under the baron's chin and shot him dead. The body was taken away in the van and chucked in a rubbish dump.

Meanwhile a million pounds was demanded in ransom. Before handing over any money, the baron's son asked the kidnapper if he could talk to his father, which of course was not possible, since he was already dead. The son was told that he could not speak directly to his father, but that his messages would be passed on. To find out whether the baron was dead or alive, the son asked the kidnapper to get his father to give him the name of his terrier from Pitmain. This dog was a well-loved Jack Russell, a gift from Bill Dey. The horrific truth was learnt when the kidnapper, unable to find out the name of the terrier, admitted that he had shot the baron. This story was reported in the national newspapers and came as a great shock to the estate workers and all who had met the baron and his family.

Bill and Angie had great faith in another terrier, called Misty. 'She bolted many a vixen out of a den,' I was told. Unfortunately Misty had only three legs: the fourth, having been caught in a gin-trap, had become gangrenous and was removed. She hopped around, but Angie took 'a hell of a shine to her'. Bill and Angie often went after foxes together with Misty and when Bill talked about her, he was always reminded of Angie's tea ritual out on the hill. At 'piece-time', having collected some wood and got a good fire going, Angie would bring out a syrup tin from his game bag and use it to boil up some water. A bit of heather stalk was added, which Bill informed me 'stopped it getting reekit [smoky] tasting', and it was boiled for four or five minutes before the tea-leaves were popped in, for the 'brewing up'. 'It was the best tea ever,' Bill remarked.

Bill also remembered Angie's old hammer gun, which had belonged to his father; he had even had a shot of it when down at the river with Angie one night. There were hoodies [hooded crows] at the ducks' eggs, but as Bill did not have his gun with him, he asked Angie to pass him his. Crossing a bog with the gun, he merely touched the trigger and both barrels went off. 'That gun was explosive!' Bill said. Many of these old guns were dangerous to handle. There were quite a few at Glentruim, but they have now all been disabled and are merely relics on the wall.

When we lived at Glentruim, Newtonmore had about fifteen shops, including two butchers. Most of these businesses have now gone. In former years, I used to wonder how there could be sufficient trade for both butchers, but there always seemed to be enough. One of them was owned by the Falconer family, who were all highly skilled in their butchering of meat and game. Stewart Falconer inherited the business from his father, but trade slackened following the construction of the new A9, when Newtonmore was bypassed. The shop was eventually sold, but by that time Stewart had become a game-dealer, providing meat to customers all over the Highlands and even further afield. Stewart was a good shot and also a keen angler, and because he was so knowledgeable about fishing and stalking as well as butchering, he knew all aspects of the sport and marketing of game.

One unforgettable day in 1990, a day that shook the whole valley, we thought we were going to lose a well-respected member of our community. It was the sort of shooting accident that all keepers assiduously seek to avoid; Stewart was the victim in this case. He had arranged to go after foxes with Bill at Pitmain. The weather had been particularly stormy over the previous days and torrential rain had caused extensive flooding, the consequence of which was that the bridge just past the parking place where they met had been washed away, leaving Pitmain marooned. This meant that Stewart had to leave his van at one side of the stream on the tarmac and then get himself to the other side, using a little makeshift crossing that Bill had built as a temporary measure.

Darkness had fallen. Bill signalled that he would set up the spotlights on the Land Rover, while Stewart went back to his van to retrieve his rifle, which was one that his father had brought back from the war, with no recoil pad. Although Stewart had already put a bullet in the chamber, the bolt was not cocked. 'This was a 99.9 per cent safe way to carry the gun,' Stewart emphasised, so what happened next was totally unpredicted.

Stewart slung the gun, on its strap, over his shoulder, but the strap broke and the gun hit the tarmac. As it landed, the impact on hard ground lifted the bolt and it fired, shooting the bullet straight up Stewart's spine. The bullet travelled up to his chest and by rights he should have been killed, but he survived. Indeed, the bullet could have killed Bill too, as he was standing not far away. By a miracle, they were both spared. Had the gun fallen on grass, the incident might not have happened; had the bridge not been washed away, they would not have been on tarmac; had the strap not broken, there would have been no accident at all. An unfortunate chain of events caused it.

Being so seriously injured, when Stewart was questioned about the accident by the police surgeon, he stated that there had been two bullets. He was not in a fit state to be coherent and what he meant was that there had been two bullets in his pocket, but the police surgeon assumed he meant that both were in the rifle. Because the investigation revealed the barrel to be empty, the police surgeon surmised that Stewart had been shot twice in the back. Bill was thus under suspicion, as Stewart could not have shot himself twice! Stewart clarified matters some time later, when he was more lucid, but in the meantime Bill was questioned incessantly.

The next three months were tough for Stewart. He remained in hospital, paralysed from the waist downwards, but to the

astonishment of all concerned, including his doctors, at least he
was still alive. One day while visiting Stewart in intensive care,
his wife thought she had noticed one of his toes moving, but was
firmly told by hospital staff that this was due to a shift in the
mattress on the bed. It happened, however, on a second occasion,
and this time the surgeon was summoned and he too agreed that
there was slight movement in one of Stewart's toes. Only a few
days later, much to the delight of all concerned, Stewart could
move one of his ankles and so it was decided to send him to Eden
Hall Hospital in Musselburgh, then considered the Scottish
equivalent of Stoke Mandeville. From that day on, there was
steady progress in Stewart's condition, every day taking him
nearer to going home.

The recovery Stewart made has been remarkable in many
ways. He was so determined to walk again that, against all odds,
he miraculously achieved this. He still has no feeling from the
waist down, yet he somehow manages to walk. However, the fact
that he does not feel extreme temperatures can be dangerous. He
was laughing when he told me a tale of driving an old soft-top
jeep down to the Chinese take-away one night, returning with the
hot meal on his knee. 'My knees were jumping all over the place,'
he said. 'I didn't realise that the supper was burning into me!'
He is even able to joke about his afflictions, to which he has
resigned himself over the years.

Because of the nature of Stewart's injuries and his amazing
subsequent progress, X-rays of the damaged spine are often
shown at seminars throughout Scotland. Looking at the X-rays
during the early days of hospitalisation, Stewart asked the
surgeon, 'Where is the bullet-head? There is only an entry
wound, but where did it exit?' He was told that it had disintegrated into tiny pieces and the lead had scattered throughout
his body on impact, and the X-rays certainly indicated that this
had happened. Yet, about a year later, Stewart had an itchy patch
on his right shoulder: the bullet, which had worked itself up

there, required a return to hospital for its removal. I was shown this trophy, kept as a reminder of how he so nearly lost his life.

Stewart gives hope to those in similar situations, who might have given up all dreams of ever walking again. His determination shows the power of his mind; what seemed impossible to others became possible. He is indeed a courageous man.

***

Shooting is an integral part of living on an estate in the Highlands and although we also organised shooting parties at Glentruim, I loved to watch the deer too much to appreciate killing them, even when culling was essential. It has been said that deer can live for an extraordinary number of years. In 1927 an article appeared in *Scottish Field* on the subject of Scottish red deer and their life-span, quoting from the works of Donald MacEachern, who wrote:

> Thrice the age of a dog, the age of a horse.
> Thrice the age of a horse, the age of a man.
> Thrice the age of a man, the age of a deer.
> Thrice the age of a deer, the age of an eagle.
> Thrice the age of an eagle, the age of an oak.

The longevity of deer had been questioned in the previous century, for in 1826, the Cameron of Lochiel of that time had shot a deer and noticed a brand-mark on the beast's ear. He asked his ghillie if he recognised the mark; he did, and five other ghillies looking at it gave the same testimony. It was well-known that a certain laird, who had been dead over 150 years, used to have his herds of deer branded in this way, and for over thirty years before his death he would habitually mark every calf. This meant that the stag that was killed could have been between 150 and 180 years old!

It is an interesting theory, but as the author of the article remarks, 'Who is there that can prove this false!' If this is truly the case, there must be incredible tales surrounding each of these magnificent creatures. I once read that high up on Bein-y-Cabhar twelve hinds were hunted by eagles, an unbelievable chase described by the keeper who witnessed it. The hinds were busy grazing at the top of the hill, and noticing that they were becoming increasingly uneasy, he scanned the sky, only to find four golden eagles flying low over the heads of the deer. The eagles proceeded to drive them, working them like sheep-dogs until they managed to separate two from the group. Continuing to swoop over them time after time, they manoeuvred their chosen two to the edge of a very steep cliff. Then followed triumph for the eagles, but disaster for the deer, as the birds drove their prey over the cliff. They fell down from a great height; one was killed and the keeper, looking through his telescope, saw the other deer make a slow, wounded escape. The light was failing, but he watched the eagles pursue their prey down into some lonely region where they would be undisturbed.

Over and over again nature can be seen to have its own way of culling, though perhaps not always in sufficient numbers for many species. Nevertheless, there will always be hunting and indeed, as a sport, it is necessary for our economy, particularly in remote parts of Scotland such as the Highlands, where tourism is the major industry.

11

Uisge Beatha

WHISKY, Scotland's national drink, is also known as uisge beatha, Gaelic for 'water of life'. In the past, Highlanders were almost expected to have a bottle of whisky in the cupboard, as was the custom at Glentruim, where our ancestors replenished the whisky decanters as soon as they were empty. The Glentruim whisky was kept in a large barrel which sat on a metal frame in the wine cellar. Whisky is a warming drink and in Scotland it has traditionally been used as a 'welcome cup', offered in a quaich, a round drinking vessel with two handles. I remember Euan taking the top off the whisky bottle and putting it aside when guests accepted their first dram, a gesture intended to be considered an invitation to stay until the bottle was finished. In previous years, the 'water of life' would have been taken regularly in the Highlands as part of healthy living and was even administered for medicinal purposes, particularly for the relief of colic. It was also thought to alleviate symptoms of smallpox and palsy.

Today a whisky trail wends its way through the heart of the Highlands, encouraging visitors to stop at different distilleries to taste a range of blends and malts. Exactly how each whisky is made is still kept secret; the individual recipes for the process have been passed down from one generation to the next. Malt whisky is claimed to have a more sophisticated flavour than the blend and distilleries producing it are found all over Scotland's mainland and islands, often built where there is easy access to the natural ingredients required for each particular local variety. The island malts have a strongly identifiable flavour and malts produced near the moors have a hint of peat in the aroma. In past centuries whisky was made over peat fires in bothies and was called 'peat-reek', probably because of the overwhelmingly tarry fumes of the peat, reek being the word for smoke in old Scots.

The art of distilling whisky in Scotland can be traced back as far as 1494, and by the sixteenth and seventeenth centuries revenues from the sale of whisky grew to such an extent that the taxman became involved. Taxes on whisky were first applied by the Scottish parliament and later through the Act of Union with England in 1707. Much to the fury of the Scots, English excise-men were sent to rout out illicit stills and bring their owners to justice. As a result, clandestine stills were hidden all over the Highlands in houses, farms, barns, crofts, bothies, caves and even under knolls. The whisky itself was concealed in secret rooms and compartments, and in all manner of other extraordinary places, such as prams, clocks, musical instruments, butter churns, drainpipes and every other kind of vessel imaginable. Furthermore, certain ministers even hid illicit stills under their pulpits, and coffins were used to smuggle whisky out of the district. Great thought went into finding locations for covert stores; in one place a tunnel was dug from an underground still to link up with a cottage chimney seventy yards away! Ladies had the benefit of their skirts, underneath which they were able to hide small barrels or even animal bladder-skins of whisky. The advantage of using these porous skins was that excess water could drain off, leaving behind a more potent spirit. This is known as the Soemmering's process. In those days whisky was sold and drunk within days of distillation, whereas today it is much more refined and takes years to mature.

Local illicit stills were the source of supply for towns and villages all over Scotland, and ponies laden with barrels were the means of transport the length and breadth of the country. The whisky carriers took great risks, but they kept alert and often carried weapons to guard their wares. One document relating to whisky smuggling describes an incident early one morning, when twenty-five Highland ponies, all tied to each other and carrying two kegs of whisky each, were observed traversing a valley, accompanied by ten or twelve men armed with bludgeons. Great lengths were taken by smugglers to deliver their whisky and keep their stills hidden from the disliked English excisemen, who neither spoke their language nor shared the same culture. At that time tax evasion was generally referred to as smuggling, so those working illicit stills were called smugglers.

Private distilling was altogether banned by parliament in 1781 and the excisemen were given the power to seize illicit whisky and smash all the equipment, calling on military manpower if necessary. This Act infuriated the Scottish people even further and made them more determined to keep what they thought was rightly theirs. The excisemen, called gaugers, were often obliged to resort to violence in their efforts to catch the smugglers and thus ensued a relentless war of wits. Illicit distillers and smugglers were invariably ready for the excisemen and would signal to each other when the officers were sighted, sometimes by lighting beacons or by waving flags from one hilltop to another.

The smugglers became efficient and organised and by the end of the eighteenth century, they were more than ready for any exciseman who dared come their way. However, legislation was passed in 1823 imposing heavy penalties on illicit distillers and also declaring it an offence for any landowner to allow the production of whisky on his land. Moreover, if a landowner was discovered harbouring smugglers on his estate, he was to be held totally responsible. Before this, landlords did not discourage their tenants or workers from possessing stills because money generated from the sale of whisky supplemented their meagre incomes, enabling them to pay their rents. It was also recognised that some of the best whisky was made by the Highland chiefs themselves for their own households. It was around this time, however, that most of the smuggling came to an end.

Dalwhinnie, a name meaning 'the meeting place', is at the heart of an area where many illicit stills are said to have formerly existed, including one beneath the kitchen floor of an old farm cottage on the nearby Glentruim Estate. There, in 1897, James Buchan founded the highest distillery in Scotland, the Strathspey, which burned down in the mid-1930s, was subsequently rebuilt and today receives many visitors from all over the world. Interestingly, there is a meteorological observation point in its grounds, from which the manager is obliged to record data of daily weather conditions from the instruments housed within a Stevenson screen, the standard casing for thermometers.

Most stills in the Highlands were owned by kindly folk, some of whom made alcohol for their own consumption only or for the purpose of barter. But a story is told about a certain smuggler of less than gentle repute, by the name of Thomas McDonald, who came from Glen Banchor, near Newtonmore. He had red hair and a fiery temper, made whisky purely for the money and was totally ruthless. Because he was heartily disliked by the locals and needed, like many others, to protect himself against the gaugers, he carried a bludgeon. It might have been necessary to own such a weapon to ward off swords or pistols, but Thomas's bludgeon was different, being studded with nails and unnecessarily barbarous.

McDonald was always one to bear a grudge and because of his violent behaviour, which was provoked by any grievance, he eventually had to leave the district. The incident which precipitated his exile occurred at a raucous, drunken party, where he fell out with a local called Ewan Rennie. Rennie came out best after the brawl, which angered his opponent so much that retaliation was inevitable. One night, knowing that Rennie would be returning to his home in Newtonmore, McDonald chose a hiding place and waited patiently for him to pass by in the dark. As soon as his victim was near, he attacked from behind, striking him with his brutal bludgeon. However, before he could smite him again, two of Rennie's neighbours happened to walk past, witnessing the fight. They were appalled by what they had seen. McDonald knew that he had been recognised and, being a marked man, too frightened to stay in the district, he made for the Trossachs as soon as he could.

A short time after his crime in Newtonmore, McDonald was once again running his own still. Although it was not the best peat-reek, he nevertheless managed to secure business in the cities and was nicknamed Tom Badenoch, after his homeland. His new friends were aware that he was an unsavoury character, but it was not until much later, when David Dougal, a gauger whom local smugglers respected for his fairness, fell victim to him, that they discovered how evil he really was. Knowing that the exciseman would be on a certain road at a certain time, and driven by utter loathing for all such officials, the smuggler had decided to lie low and trap him. After all, whisky was of the utmost importance to him and anyone who might jeopardise his business was his enemy.

That night Dougal was patrolling his district when he came across Badenoch, who was obviously prepared for him, for he was holding a pistol. Although he could not see any whisky around, he knew that it would be there somewhere. Dougal himself was not armed, but he risked holding up his spyglass as a substitute for a gun and ordered Badenoch to surrender. Badenoch, thinking the tax-man was indeed holding a gun, took a shot but missed, then promptly took off in the other direction. On scanning the area, Dougal happened to notice a pony tethered nearby, laden with whisky, and so, without hesitation, he grabbed the mare and attaching her to his own horse, led her back to town, whisky and all. Gossip travelled fast and soon everyone discovered that Badenoch had been fooled by the gauger with a spyglass. Badenoch, his pride wounded, was livid and hatred for Dougal festered in his mind for months. Vengeance was inevitable.

Weeks and weeks went by, yet nothing happened. Then a young cowherd saw a bundle of rags on the ground as he was driving his cows along a country path near Callander. On further inspection, he realised it was not in fact a bundle of rags, but a body that had been battered almost beyond recognition. The corpse was that of Dougal and it was apparent that he had been bludgeoned to death by a brutal instrument, which must have had sharp projections, such as nails.

Subsequent investigation concluded that Dougal had been killed elsewhere, his body having been transported to the spot where he was found. Weeks later Dougal's spyglass, knife and wallet were retrieved near a small lochan, miles up in the hills to the north. Everyone knew that Badenoch was the murderer and after this heinous, brutal crime he was ignored by all. Not a soul would give him the time of day. Loathed by his fellow men, he became solitary, wandering aimlessly through the foothills of Perthshire until he was seen no more.

The following spring a decomposed body was found on the slopes of Ben Vorlich and beside the body lay a nail-studded bludgeon. This also happened to be the place where the spyglass, knife and wallet had been found. With nowhere to go and not a soul in the world to confide in, perhaps Badenoch had no choice but to go back to the scene of the crime to seek repentance.

***

Fifty years ago the Speyside Whisky Distillery, a private enterprise, was established locally. It was built by George and Susan Christie on a somewhat neglected estate they had found up the Strath at Old Milton, which is reached by the back road from Kingussie to Rothiemurchus, directly opposite Balavil on the far side of the valley. They acquired old stone for the walls, bringing in truckloads of granite and sandstone for that purpose and also to repair all the dykes on the estate. Barley was brought in and spread across the malting floors, after which it was dampened until it was completely soaked, and so the process of making whisky began. George told me that in those early days whisky was actually cheap to make, costing about 4 s. 6 d. (20p) per gallon, which included paying wages. He said, however, that although five people could make 300,000 gallons of blend per year, the production of malt whisky was a good deal slower. Their output was tanked and taken to Alloa, near Glasgow, where it was put into wooden barrels to mature for three or four years before it could be regarded as viable whisky. The Christies were never really interested in opening their premises to the public, considering their distillery a strictly family concern.

Those were the days when whisky was part of life, yet could take over many lives in a potentially disastrous way. Stories on the subject of whisky drinking are legion in the Highlands, for nowhere was untouched by uisge beatha. Certain tales from the northern end of the valley sum up the general humour arising from this form of indulgence.

In the 1960s, Wilma Riley used to run the Heatherbrae Hotel in Nethybridge, an era she looked back on as the most eventful of her life. She described the back bar of the Nethy Hotel as a 'dirty smelly bar' (it was then known as Budge's Bar, after the barman), and it was like living in the Wild West. To illustrate, she told me about the occasion when she actually rode into Budge's Bar on her pony, but no one batted an eyelid: there were no strange looks, not even a glance up from the whisky-filled glasses.

Wilma came from a colourful family herself, her mother having been a Tiller girl, latterly married to one of the Crazy Gang. Her real father had also been in showbusiness – he was a comedian known as Billy Bennett – but he had died when she was eleven. Her house was full of theatrical and showbiz memorabilia, old records and pictures.

'It was a village of poachers, sometimes quite lawless,' Wilma continued. 'There were tourists playing darts one night in the bar and they asked where the double five or double two was on the board. A local piped up, "I'll show you where it is," and with that he lifted his shot-gun and fired at the board, hitting it dead on double five.' The board disintegrated and the regulars in the bar gave a standing ovation, which left the visitors rather bewildered.

'There was always something going on in Budge's Bar,' Wilma continued, launching into one of her many tales. 'Someone came in one evening trying to sell a chainsaw, and a prospective buyer asked him if it worked. "I'll show you how it f***ing works," was the reply. He did show him how it worked: he sawed the table in half!'

Then there was the local grave-digger. He came into Wilma's bar in the Heatherbrae one night, with a skull tucked under his arm. The skull was placed on the bar and its living mate told her that his friend needed a drink. He was a character, but had not quite perfected his job over the years, for he never dug the holes large enough. At funeral services he had to have his spade with him, ready for digging out a little more to accommodate the coffin.

Everyone enjoyed a drink and seemed to get away with it in those days. Quite often the mail bags would be abandoned in the Gents, while the two postmen merrily drank away the evening in the bar of the Heatherbrae Hotel. Following one such session, the cleaner found a set of teeth in the Gents the next morning. The staff all stared hard at them and then in unison remarked, 'They're Ian's teeth!' Ian was one of the postmen. While they were in mid-discussion on the subject of the teeth, in walked Ian, toothless. 'Anyone seen my teeth?' he mumbled, just before he was happily reunited with his choppers.

The locals were lawless in the pub and lawless on the road, it seemed. Those were the days you were asked to walk the line in the middle of the road, to ascertain whether you could walk straight; if not, you had had too much to drink. However, once off the main road there was no white line in those parts. Wilma told me about a certain local who drove what she referred to as 'a beat-up little van'. He had offered her a lift early one morning as she walked up the road on her way back from the baker's, her arms laden with fresh bread. She later regretted accepting, for the driver was blazing drunk. They were stopped by a policeman, who originated from the West Coast, and in his soft Highland accent he politely asked the driver to step out of the car. 'Get out, you are just making a fool of me,' said the policeman. 'And you come out too,' he ordered the passenger. 'You can drive.' The dashboard was missing in this jalopy and there was no obvious way of starting the car. When Wilma asked how to start the engine, she was told to pull on two wires! There was no key and certainly no seat-belts, nor indeed was there a breathalyser or any sort of caution: the policeman just turned a blind eye. It wouldn't happen today.

In the 1960s the railways dominated the area. The diesel train which carried the barrels of whisky up to Aviemore was called *Sputnic* and the engine driver, 'Tootie'. The whisky train seemed prone to execute dangerous manoeuvres, for it had been known to plough through the level-crossing gates at Nethy Bridge and shunt through the engine shed at Boat of Garten, and even managed to derail one of its trucks at Aviemore, causing havoc with the London trains. Needless to say, three misadventures were too many to go unnoticed, particularly since the third one affected London, and so Tootie, *Sputnic*'s driver, was suspended. 'Ah well, it would be the whisky,' locals observed.

Much of the whisky was stolen after it had been loaded onto the trains, often by means of holes drilled under the wagons so that the spirit could be siphoned out from the barrels on board. There was a lot of whisky-thieving at that time; at Aviemore all sorts of containers would be filled with whisky from the barrels in transit, including the station's watering-cans.

The valley of the whisky trail has moved on from the days when there were peat-reekers and gaugers. Smuggling and thieving has been exchanged for carefree days of mere overindulgence. Higher taxes may now have an influence on sales, but as is the tradition, there will always be a welcome in the Highlands in the form of a dram.

12

Ruthven

THERE is a long history behind the tales of Ruthven. In the thirteenth century a castle was built on the outskirts of Kingussie, of which the Revd Lachlan Shaw, historian of the Province of Moray, who died in 1777, wrote, 'The Castle of Ruthven, the seat of Comyn Lord Badenoch, stood on a green mount tapering to the top, as if it were artificial; the area on the top, about 100 yards long and 30 broad; the south wall was 9 feet thick, through which the arched entry was guarded by a double iron grate, and a port-cullis; the other walls were 16 feet high, and 4 thick, and in the north end of the court were two towers in the corners, and some low buildings, and a draw-well within the court.' This castle was the first of several built on the same site, but not much is mentioned about the others, except for the last, which provided little protection from the wind and rain. The accommodation in this semi-ruin was so poor that soldiers deserted and incessant rain affected the health of those who remained, for they contracted flux, scurvy and other diseases.

Walter Comyn, alias Black Comyn, had two estates, one at Blair Athol and the other at Ruthven, and used to travel between the two by way of Cumming's Road. This road, sometimes called the Wine Road, was named after its maker and was originally built so that wine carts could pass easily to and from each district. Comyn had feudal rights on his land and, much to the disgust of the local Highlanders, he expected labour and services in part-payment for rent. A cruel and vicious man, he was feared by all his tenants and also had a reputation with the ladies, drifting from one conquest to the next. One day his messenger, Red Murdoch (Muriach Ruadh), also a tyrant, rode out from the castle with an armed guard and trumpeters to impose a despicable order on the people of Ruthven. They panicked when they saw him coming and ran into their houses to hide. Arriving at the centre of the village, the party halted and the trumpets were given a blast, to attract attention. Red Murdoch issued his message: all women between the ages of twelve and thirty years were to work naked in the fields when shearing the corn. This order was to be carried out three days later, when Comyn would be riding past, checking on his labourers and their work. The women were gripped with fear and their men were furious, but they knew that they would have to obey or risk losing their lives. One particularly attractive young girl, petrified because she knew that Red Murdoch had an unhealthy interest in her, asked her sweetheart's advice, knowing that he in turn would speak to his grandmother, who was reputed to be a witch. The young girl was told not to worry, for the old lady's response was, 'Have no fears: neither Black Comyn nor Red Murdoch will live to see the day.'

The morning before the shearing, Comyn announced his intention to ride with some of his men from his lowland estate to meet Red Murdoch, who would also come on horseback with his men from Ruthven Castle; they would meet halfway. They made the rendezvous, but none of the men was ever seen alive again. The Badenoch people saw a horse galloping in terror towards Ruthven Castle, with torn strips of one of Comyn's legs and a foot lodged in the stirrup; the rest of his body was allegedly found strewn in shreds all round Gaick. Some locals firmly believed that two witches, in the form of eagles, had attacked Comyn, throwing him from his horse and then devouring his body, leaving behind trails of tissue hanging from the horse's saddle.

Others thought that it might have been the menfolk, enraged by the way Comyn treated their women, who had taken revenge. A petrified horse, carrying pieces of flesh and a foot, was found in a lowland glen, known ever since as Ruigh Leth-chois, meaning 'shieling of the one foot'. There is also a version of this gruesome tale which relates that it was Red Murdoch who was mangled, and that bits of him hung from the saddle of his horse as it galloped back to the gates of Ruthven Castle. In addition, there were said to have been signs of a deadly battle in a narrow valley in the wilds of Gaik called The Pass of the Comyns. Fragments of clothes and dismembered bodies were found where Comyn and his whole party of men were allegedly killed. Whichever account was true, none is particularly edifying. We shall never know what really took place.

Alexander Stewart, Alisdair Mor mac an Righ, born in 1342, was the great-grandson of Robert the Bruce and the son of King Robert II. He lived in numerous fortresses throughout Scotland, including Ruthven Castle in Badenoch and Loch an Eilein Castle at Rothiemurchus. He held the lordship of Badenoch and, around 1371, he also became the earl of Buchanan, but he was more commonly remembered as the Wolf of Badenoch or Big Alexander. He was one of the more notorious historical characters of Strathspey, a violent man capable of rape, arson and even murder. The inhabitants of the lands he ruled certainly feared him, for if they so much as displeased the Wolf of Badenoch, he would ransack and torch their homes.

When he deserted his wife, the countess of Ross, in favour of his mistress, he was excommunicated from the Church by the Bishop of Moray. He was outraged by this decision, believing that the Church was trying to confiscate land which was rightly his, and therefore he took revenge, burning down Elgin Cathedral as well as Pluscarden Abbey. The king knew about his son's atrocities and, after his excommunication, tried to make Alexander repent for his sins. Although he was eventually pardoned by his father and accepted back into the Church, it is said that his vow was short-lived and he fell back into his old wicked ways.

There have been many dates given for the death of the Wolf but it is now thought that it was between 1405 and 1406. Legend has it that on his last night at Ruthven Castle, the Wolf of Badenoch opened the door to a tall, dark man dressed in black and the two men played chess together for several hours, until the visitor made a move and called out 'check', then 'checkmate'. At that moment there was a terrible thunderclap, accompanied by lightning, and the storm continued throughout the night. In the morning the Wolf of Badenoch's men were found lying outside the castle walls, all of them dead and their bodies charred, as if struck by lightning, whereas the corpse of the Wolf of Badenoch was discovered in the dining-hall without a mark upon it, although the nails of his boots had been torn out. The local people surmised that he had been playing chess with the Devil himself the night before.

Those terrible storms blew up again on the day of the Wolf of Badenoch's funeral. His coffin was borne at the front of the procession and the storm that erupted was extremely violent, but when the coffin was taken to the back of the procession, the storm abated. Before he died, the Wolf of Badenoch had once more repented of his transgressions and again was pardoned by his father. He was buried in Dunkeld Cathedral, where his effigy can still be seen today.

Another ancient tale from the district of Ruthven involves a forester who served in Argyll's army and was believed to have a leannan sith, a fairy sweetheart, who appeared in the form of a white hind and followed him everywhere. The troops became used to seeing the hind, but were curious as to why Argyll had not had her shot. One day, therefore, while resting in the region of Ruthven Castle, they asked him if there was a specific reason for not taking this hind. He disliked the manner in which he was questioned and in his fury, immediately ordered his men to raise their rifles and fire at the deer. All fired, except for the forester, who aimed but only pretended to shoot. Argyll, noticing this, once more gave him the order, but the reply he received was, 'I will fire at your command, Argyll, but it will be the last shot that I will ever fire.' No bullet actually hit the deer, but the fairy gave out a terrific scream as her apparition floated up the mountain side in a patch of mist. As the troops watched the leannan sith in disbelief, the forester, who had fired with great reluctance, dropped down dead. Neither his fairy sweetheart nor the white hind was ever seen again.

***

In the eighteenth century, Kingussie school was situated somewhere in the vicinity of the barracks and Ruthven farm. The building would have been primitive, since most dwellings in those days were turf huts, constructed with couples, now often called crucks. These were A-shaped, load-bearing roof timbers, across which lay pans (lighter timbers) at right angles; thatch-bearing cabers were then placed over the pans parallel to the underling couples, or crucks. Tossing the caber became an important element of Highland games.

Between 1754 and 1758 a very young master named James Macpherson taught at the school. Macpherson was also known by his friends as Seumas Ban, 'fair-haired James'. He was described in the latter part of the last century by George Dixon, who is originally from Grantown-on-Spey and is an authority on the history of the district, as 'by far the most famous – not to say infamous – schoolmaster ever to have taught in either Badenoch or Strathspey'. For part of each year James would teach his classes close to the gutted barracks, where he himself had once been a pupil. His salary was drawn from the impoverished local estates, the Macpherson chief's part of which had been forfeited after the Rebellion of 1745. As a parochial schoolmaster, James therefore received a pittance, which made him despondent. It was perhaps this factor that fired his eagerness to seek a more lucrative source of income when he ventured further south to seek his fortune. According to Dixon, records show that Macpherson appears to have put himself through university courses in Aberdeen and Edinburgh during the winter months, thus furthering his career, instead of continuing his teaching at the school.

One of James' boyhood friends met him on a walk one day and asked him why he looked so depressed. James answered that he was tired of being a mere schoolmaster, but did not know how to better himself. It did not take long before his world changed in the way that he had longed for and he became both famous and wealthy. During his rise to fame, he involved himself in politics, was an agent for Mohamet Ali, the Nabob of Arcot, and ultimately became a Member of Parliament. James certainly had an interesting career, mostly in literary endeavour, his main interest being poetry. He gained a certain notoriety, as well as the sobriquet of 'Ossian' Macpherson, because of what were later criticised as his dubious translations of the old Gaelic poems of Ossian, which he claimed to have found.

Lachlan Macpherson of Strathmashie, a learned Gaelic scholar who lived further to the south of Ruthven, assisted James with these translations and it is thought by some that James added material to ancient fragments of Ossian's poetry to make the work more suitable for the market at the time. It is interesting to read the views of Elizabeth Grant of Rothiemurchus on the subject of Ossian Macpherson. Writing in the nineteenth century about one of James' sons in her *Memoirs*, she tartly remarks, 'Belleville was the son of Ossian, of the Macpherson who pretended to translate Ossian, and made a fine fortune out of the Nabob of Arcot's debts. Who this Macpherson was I do not rightly know. A lad of parts, however, though of very lowly birth, not even a little farmer's son.' She also added that he never married.

James' finances must have improved dramatically, since by 1788 he could afford to employ the fashionable architect Robert Adam to design and build Belleville for him. Now an affluent landowner, he found himself looking across from his new mansion on the outskirts of Kingussie to Ruthven, where as a young schoolmaster he had taught in a turf hut in the 1750s. He was also a contemporary of the notorious Captain Macpherson, known as the Black Officer, who had negotiated several lairdships in the parish for him, including Phoness, an estate not far from Glentruim.

Long ago, it was not an uncommon belief in the Highlands that a woman could take the form of a deer. In the Highland Folk museum at Kingussie there is even an article about Ossian which states that some thought Ossian's mother had been a hind, whilst others believed that he had been nurtured by a deer! It was said that this did not come to light until it was noticed that he persistently refused to eat venison!

Whether James wrote part of the Ossian poems or translated them in their entirety from the original Gaelic does not really matter: he gave the English-speaking world access to this otherwise obscure literature. In agreement Dixon wrote, 'No more widely influential Highlander has lived in recent centuries than that particular Kingussie schoolmaster. As the writer who above all others made the Highlands respectable and attractive for the southern visitor, Macpherson – however fraudulently, and however unintentionally as regards his fabrications' ultimate effect – became a foundation stone of the modern Highland tourist industry and so of the present Highland economy.' His work was renowned and he was honoured for the part he played in the publication of the Ossian poems. He was so highly respected that he was buried in Poets' Corner in Westminster Abbey in 1796 and his mahogany coffin is reputed to have two linings, one of Glenfeshie fir, the other of lead. A marble obelisk commemorating this famous

Macpherson stands in the grounds of his house, which is now known as Balavil.

★★★

From 1719, five centuries after Ruthven Castle was first built, the Hanoverian Government constructed four regular garrisons at strategic locations throughout the Highlands, each holding 120 infantrymen. Amongst these essential defences was Ruthven Barracks, where, in August 1745, Sergeant Malloy and twelve redcoats managed to ward off an attack of over 200 Jacobites. Only one soldier was lost, shot through the head because he had dared to raise it above the parapet. After Culloden, however, some of the defeated Jacobites retreated to Ruthven, later receiving the news there that the Rebellion was over and Prince Charles Edward Stuart had fled to France. In 1746 Prince Charlie's army rallied for the last time at the barracks, then disbanded and set fire to the building. Only the stable blocks and an impressive shell remain today to remind visitors of its intriguing history as they pass through Badenoch.

Ruthven Barracks, built on the site of an early medieval castle, stands in a stark valley surrounded by sweeping hills. This picturesque landscape provides a dramatic backdrop redolent of the fortress's grim history, palpably evoking tales of countless blood-curdling incidents, however apocryphal they may have become in the telling over the years. I have been to moonlit ceilidhs at that desolate place, when harp, fiddle and bagpipes could be heard ringing out their tunes for miles, the music rebounding from the hills, leaving behind a delicate, shimmering echo. On one such occasion, I remember the audience standing beneath the barracks in the twilight, totally entranced by the atmosphere. Flames from torches perched high on the parapets sharply defined the outline of the ruins against the horizon, presenting a spectacle poetic enough to stir the imagination of even the least susceptible of those present.

13

The Souterrain

GEORGE Dixon was briefly a history teacher at Alford in Aberdeenshire and was also an intermittent contributor over several decades to the *Strathspey and Badenoch Herald*. After years of research in manuscript sources in Edinburgh, he had custody at one time of the historical records of half a dozen Scottish local authorities, latterly as Regional Archivist in Central Region. He is well-known for his extensive knowledge of the district of Badenoch and Strathspey, and his interesting views on its history and legends.

In 1955 George visited a Pictish souterrain, a subterranean earth house in Raitts, near Ruthven. It consists of a single long, curved chamber lined with drystone walls and roofed with slabs of stone. The entrance was originally a narrow hole in the ground at one end, leading gently downwards into the slightly wider but still restricted space of the souterrain. The earth house, now assumed to be an Iron Age structure, was known in the eighteenth century as the Cave of the Nine Robbers or the Cave of McNivens (Clanan Ichilnew), who became enemies of the Cluny Macphersons. It was said that the quarrel began when land was taken from the McNivens by Robert the Bruce to give to the Macphersons, who had supported him, and when the Macphersons claimed it, the McNivens stole their cattle. To avoid any conflict, the Macphersons sent their daughter to persuade them to give back their cows, but she returned having been badly treated, with her petticoats torn and the bull without its tongue. Revenge was inevitable, so the MacNiven sons fled to the souterrain, which was an ideal place to hide, for a house had been built on top. The Macphersons, determined to seek them out, sent one of their men as a spy, disguised with a beard and beggar's clothes. He arrived at the door of the house and was kindly offered food and a bed for the night, but not wishing to arouse suspicion, he refused the bed, only accepting the nourishment. Late into the evening, still lacking information, he decided to feign illness as a means to prolong his stay. He pretended to be in agony with a complaint called gravel disease, rightly predicting that his hostess would take pity on him and kindly offer him a peat bed in front of the fire. When the lady of the house thought he was asleep, she carried on with her evening's work, making oatcakes, unaware that the stranger was still awake and watching her bake batch after batch, which she carefully put away in a cupboard. Having noticed that the oatcakes seemed to vanish as soon as the cupboard was filled, he realised that there must be a secret room beneath the dwelling. The informer left as soon as he could, to notify the Cluny Macphersons of his findings. Thus the McNivens were ambushed by the Macphersons and taken out to be hanged on a nearby tree or beheaded on a block by the door. Either way, their end was unpleasant. The lady of the house was also killed and the house pulled down. Revenge came in a mysterious form, for after this brutal attack members of the Cluny family were afflicted with the same complaint that the spy had faked!

★★★

All over the Highlands you will still hear of the fairies, places where they tend to linger and gifts that they can bestow on humans. There is a story about a John MacNiven, a crofter, who was married to Meg Mhor, meaning Big Meg. They too lived

124

near Ruthven and were very content with their lives, except for one thing – they had no sons, only two daughters. Desperate for sons, Big Meg would have done anything in her power to enable them to carry on the family name.

There are different opinions about what fairies wear. Some think that they only dress in green, but others imagine that they have seen them clad in the same colour as lichen, as well as plants of other hues on the hills and heaths. Meg had learnt from old folk that you could only see fairies when they had no clothes on at all, and she had also been told that if you could catch a fairy, you would be granted three wishes that would come true. She was aware of a fairy knoll near her house, because she had often seen fairies there, playing and dancing in the moonlight. She intended to make her wish for a son come true, so decided to catch one of the fairies while they were all down at the burn washing their clothes. When they took off their garments to wash them, she would try to catch one in her hand, before they dressed themselves and became invisible again. Meg was successful and managed to catch a fairy. The little creature pleaded with her to let her go and offered her three wishes in exchange for her freedom. Her wishes were for sons, to be a skilled spinner and for her cows to be good milkers. All her wishes were granted and the fairy escaped from between Meg's large fingers and, quickly gathering up her clothes, became invisible and fluttered away.

The MacNivens were blessed with seven healthy sons, Meg became an expert spinner and their cows produced top-class milk. Their sons became athletes and the next generation of sons followed in their father's footsteps, being talented runners.

The last son to be born in that family was Domhnall Dubh, 'Black Donald', who was disgraced because of desertion from the Black Watch. The Black Officer, who was in charge of recruitment, managed to capture Donald in Newtonmore and lock him up in Kingussie jail. He was to take his prisoner to Inverness, but on the journey Donald managed to persuade him that he was a changed man and was now in favour of the army. Taken in by Donald's cunning words, the Black Officer allowed the men to remove his handcuffs so that he could have a dram. At the first chance, Donald escaped and fled to Gaick Forrest, where he hid alone for some time. Eventually he managed to persuade an old friend to give him shelter, but he knew that the reward offered for his arrest would be too tempting for anyone to resist. He was therefore not surprised when his friend took him out one night to hide in his barn and turned the key on him. Donald knew instinctively what to expect and hid in the shadows of the barn, waiting for the Black Officer to come looking for him. When the door was opened, Donald knew he was well hidden and felt safe, but unfortunately he coughed, which drew the attention of the Black Officer. 'You heard me, but you can't see me; if you saw me, you couldn't find me; if you found me, you couldn't catch me, and if you caught me, you couldn't hold me.' Those were the words Donald shouted from his dark, hidden corner, and then he was away, never to return.

***

Within the lands of Raitts, on the site where Balavil was eventually built, once stood a house dating from the sixteenth century. It later belonged to Mackintosh of Borlum, who, after a colourful career, became a brigadier in the Jacobite Army during the uprising known as the Fifteen (1715). Following defeat, he was observed to cut an outstanding figure among the other rebels as they were marched to London, advanced in years though he was. According to the historian Burton, 'Brigadier Mackintosh, remarkable for the grim ferocity of his scarred face, attracted in captive procession glances which, through the influence of his formidable presence, had in them more respect than ridicule, even from the exulting crowd.'

He was indicted for high treason and imprisoned at Newgate, but escaped on the eve of his trial. He longed to return to his homelands and often did, staying with his son Shaw, pretending to be a cousin. However, the commandant of Ruthven Castle became suspicious about the 'visiting cousin' and early one morning took six of his men to Raitts in search of the brigadier. The officer's suspicions were well-founded: the brigadier was 'surprised in his dressing-gown and slippers' and arrested forthwith. However, when the local people got wind of the arrest, they rallied round, broke into the house and challenged the soldiers. The brigadier quickly made his escape and had four years of freedom before he was finally captured, spending the last fifteen years of his life in Edinburgh Castle, where he died in 1743.

Mackintosh of Borlum was a learned agriculturist and in 1729 anonymously published a pioneering work on agricultural improvement. In it he lamented the 'epidemick' of extravagance which had evolved since the Union and placed Scotland 'in the situation of a family that expends more within doors than our industry without supplies . . . Where I once saw a gentleman, lady and children dress'd clean and neat in home-spun stuffs, of her own sheep's growth and women's spinning, I see now English broadcloth. Where I saw the table serv'd in Scots clean fine linen, I see now Flemish and Dutch diaper and damask. And where, with two or three substantial dishes of beef, mutton and fowl, garnish'd with their own wholesome gravy I see now serv'd up several services of little expensive ashets, with English pickles, yea Indian mangoes, and catch-up or anchovy sauces.' These changes do not solely belong to that era; the same could be said today.

Borlum's wife had moved in high circles before she married; she had been a maid of honour to Queen Anne. She continued to live at Raitts, which she had previously inherited from the brigadier's father, until she died at the early age of forty-four. Her family felt that the difficulty of her existence there in comparison to the grandeur she had experienced in the south contributed to her early death.

127

Mackintosh of Borlum and his wife had two sons, Lachlan and Shaw, and it is probable that the boys were educated at the parochial school of Kingussie in Ruthven village. Lachlan, the eldest, inherited Raitts from his mother, although he did not stay in the area. He emigrated to Rhode Island, where he married and had two daughters, but unfortunately he drowned at sea on his way back to Scotland for a visit. Much to the annoyance of his younger brother Shaw, a villainous character, Raitts passed to Lachlan's two daughters. Shaw, determined to acquire the place that he was used to calling home, sailed across the Atlantic in search of his two nieces, aged thirteen and fourteen, who by then were living with friends in Boston. He planned to take custody of these children, who barred his inheritance of Raitts. Having failed to cajole the girls into returning with him by demonstrations of affection and consideration for their welfare, he resorted to the law, which proved unhelpful. He was therefore driven to resolve his case by devious means. He hired a gang of ruffians to kidnap and smuggle them on board the vessel in which he himself was to return to Scotland. However, moments before they were about to sail, the girls were rescued and taken back to Boston, while Shaw was arrested and imprisoned, narrowly escaping being lynched. On payment of a bond of £2000 and with a promise to abstain from any further molestation of his nieces, he was released. Nobody knew what he had planned to do with them, but one can only surmise that his intentions were far from honourable.

Shaw's only legitimate son, Edward Shaw Mackintosh of Borlum, known as Ned, also had a merciless streak. At a very early age, he headed a lawless gang 'which infested the Highland roads as highwaymen'. One of his favourite haunts was the Pass of Slochd Muick on the way to Inverness, where he and his men used to lie low, ready to pounce on travellers, robbing and murdering them as they tried to pass. A pool between Belleville and Dunachton was said to be the scene of

128

one of his murders. In 1773 the *Aberdeen Journal* reported the outlawing of Ned, as well as the trial of his brother and another member of his gang of highway robbers, under the heading 'Circuit Court at Inverness'.

Then came on before the Court a Trial of a very singular Nature, for Crimes which we hope for the Honour of humanity will never be heard of again: these were no other than an Association to rob and murder Passengers on the High-way. The Persons indicted, were Edward Shaw Mackintosh of Borlum, Alexander Mackintosh his natural Brother, John Forbes, Miller at Mill of Reats, William Davidson in Beldow of Reats, and Evan Dow Maclauchlan, and Donald Dow Robertson, both Servants to Borlum. All except Alexander Mackintosh and William Davidson had fled, and were therefore outlawed: and the Trial against the other two lasted till one in the Morning, when the Jury inclosed, and returned their Verdict at nine, all in one Voice, finding Mackintosh guilty art and part of the Crimes lybelled, except stealing the Bear from Mr Blair, and by a plurality of Voices, Davidson guilty art and part of the Crime of robbing the House of James McPherson, Weaver in Laggan of Killihuntly. They were both sentenced to be hanged at Inverness the second day of July next, and the Body of Alexander Mackintosh to be hung in chains. It came out on the trial against this gang, that they had graves ready dug for the reception of such unfortunate victims as should fall in their Way.

After the trial, the Edinburgh papers recorded the following:

On Friday July 2, was hanged at Inverness, and his body afterwards hung in chains, Alexander Mackintosh, natural brother to Edward Shaw Mackintosh of Borlum, for the apprehension of whom a reward of 50 s. 1 d. was lately offered. Alexander Mackintosh was condemned at the last circuit court of Justiciary held at Inverness, along with William Davidson who [has] since received his Majesty's pardon, as formerly mentioned, for having been guilty of robbery, and entering into an association to murder and rob passengers on the high-way, with Borlum, and several other persons, who were all fugitate for not appearing to stand trial.

The court case took place in 1773, but Ned had already absconded, never to be seen again.

Long after the disappearance of her husband, Ned's wife, whose brother was Duncan Macpherson of Breakachy, left Raitts, which was confiscated by the Crown, represented by the duke of Gordon and then sold to James (Ossian) Macpherson in 1788. Brought up as a privileged lady, she desperately tried to live once more in the style to which she had been accustomed before her marriage to Borlum. Although her income was modest, she was determined to have a social life and mix with the right people. The locals were amused by what they considered to be her pretensions, particularly on the occasion she was invited to a ball given by the Duchess of Gordon at Kinrara in honour of Prince Leopold of Belgium. Lacking a carriage of her own, she arrived by horse and cart, putting on a brave face despite desertion by a husband who had left a trail of dishonour in his wake.

In those days there was a ferry across the river from Ruthven to Balavil, joining the main thoroughfare north, which then passed through Raitts. Travellers on that highway must have been easy prey for the McNiven robbers, whose house was very close to the road at that time. Today all that remains is an outline of the house, but the souterrain is still there and it is also probable that there are other early settlements in the area still waiting to be excavated.

14

The Cairngorms

AVIEMORE, on the north-west side of the Cairngorm mountains, has become a major centre for skiing in Scotland. From the 1950s, numerous ski schools of various kinds sprang up in the surrounding area as the sport gained popularity. The origins of such enterprise and the ensuing prosperity can be traced back to the arrival of a group of Norwegian soldiers in the area to practise their skiing techniques during the Second World War. Their alpine company, incidentally, was named after one Captain Linge, who had been killed while engaged in sabotage against German installations in occupied Norway.

Local people still vividly remember the young men walking through the streets of Grantown-on-Spey and neighbouring villages, distinctive in their white camouflage uniforms. A few years later, many of the ex-soldiers returned to visit old haunts and rekindle friendships, amongst them Colonel Sandvik, who suggested that skiers from Norway should come over to start up a ski school. An Austrian, Karl Fuchs, a fully qualified ski instructor already living in Carrbridge, who had just begun to teach his sport in the valley, combined forces with Colonel Sandvik to make contact with the ski school in Oslo. Odd Gulbrandsen, the secretary of the Norwegian Ski School, said he would help and so a string of hand-picked skiers made their way to Scotland to instruct. One of them, Eilif Moen, became the first chief instructor and director. However, because it was very difficult to obtain a work permit, one potential instructor tried to enter the country illegally, pretending to be on holiday, only to be turned away at Newcastle docks. A year or so later, in 1956, a number of Norwegian students were eventually recruited and employed to assist with running the new establishment, which became known as the Scottish–Norwegian Ski School, which was then based in Grantown.

It must have been tough for skiers when the schools were first set up, for there were no chairlifts. The depth of snow was much greater than it is today: one had to be very keen and also fit to make the journey to the top on foot. As well as the lack of chairlifts, there were also no other facilities. Eilif told me about an amusing incident when he, along with six other instructors, took a class of beginners up the slopes in the early days. Around lunchtime one of the ladies was desperate to relieve herself, but with no public conveniences on site, she was told to go behind a very large boulder. As instructed, with her skis still on her feet, she ventured over to the rock and disappeared behind it. Because the terrain was not exactly level, she had trouble balancing and therefore struggled to divest herself of certain garments. Finally settling into a comfortable position, to her horror she found herself gently gliding out on her skis from behind the boulder. Her screams alerted the whole of the class, drawing attention to her misfortune. Luckily, two of the female instructors went to her rescue and the male instructors, realising the woman's predicament, stood close together with their backs to her, forming a shield.

There was a lot of activity in the valley at that time and the Speyside Hoteliers group began a fundraising exercise to raise money for roads and chairlifts, so that skiers could be taken up to the Lecht and to the foot of the White Lady in the Cairngorms. The chairlifts were essential if skiers were to be attracted to the area and an access road was just as necessary. The improvements would be costly, so money was raised to build a road from Glenmore up to the car park: £5,000 in Grantown alone, and the association of Speyside Hoteliers, which included Alistair McIntyre from the Carrbridge Hotel, brought the total to £15,000, the sum required. Once the target had been met, the County Council agreed to take over maintenance of the new road. Unfortunately, shortly after it had been completed, disaster struck: a bridge and part of the road were washed away in the aftermath of horrendous weather. This prolonged the timescale of the whole project, for the road from Glenmore to the car park had to be rebuilt.

A chairlift was the next goal for the fund-raising committee, but having already spent a huge amount of money on the first stage of the work, the remainder seemed impossible to achieve. However, an extraordinary turn of events saved the day. As luck would have it, Jock Kerr-Hunter, who worked with the Scottish Council for Physical Recreation, which later became the Sports Council, was in his office when a stranger walked in. This unexpected visitor happened to be a very wealthy tea planter, who wished to donate money to sport. After discussing the plans for the chairlift, the gentleman agreed to match pound for pound the required £40,000. Very nearly £20,000 was raised and, much to the astonishment of the Council, when the benefactor was told that there was a bit of a shortfall, he announced that he would pay the entire balance. What a day that must have been! The top chairlift was built first, in 1961, which meant that people had to walk up to the middle station, until the lower part was constructed some years later. However, regardless of its limitations, the ski resort had been established and soon the locals saw many visitors using the new facilities. It was all thanks to the very generous donor, who wished to remain anonymous.

The Cairngorm Winter Sports Development Board, later called The Chairlift Company, was formed with Major Archie Scott as chairman, Colin Sutton (who used to manage the

Craiglynne Hotel in Grantown-on-Spey) as secretary and Bob Clyde as general manager. They and their colleagues were involved from the outset and were instrumental in opening up part of the Highlands to thousands of tourists, promoting skiing as a popular sport and generating valued revenue for the whole Speyside area.

Many people have got lost or even died on the Cairngorm mountain range, for weather conditions on its exposed, desolate flanks and summits are notoriously unpredictable. A day that begins in warm sunshine may well end in dangerous blizzards. To illustrate, Colin told me the grim tale of a man who had arrived at his hotel about forty years ago, looking for his daughter and her boyfriend. He asked whether they had stayed there that weekend and said that although their car had been found at the foot of the mountains, they were nowhere to be seen. The Mountain Rescue Team did not yet exist, but members of the Scottish Ski Club who happened to be around at the time volunteered to go out and look for them.

Every weekend for six weeks they searched for the young couple, but only after the snow had melted were the bodies found, first that of the girl and later the young man, on a mountainside halfway to Tomintoul. Though the weather had been good when they set off, it must have turned menacingly wild, making them lose their way. It looked as if they had walked over the summit, probably descending in the direction of Tomintoul to follow the river from Loch Avon, which they perhaps thought would guide them back to civilisation. However, there was no shelter on this route and they would have been fatally exposed to the fierce blizzards.

Fred Crayke was the officer in charge of Aviemore Police Station and when there were accidents in the hills, he had to find fit and able men to turn out as quickly as possible. With the increase in advertising encouraging tourists to visit the Cairngorms, it was inevitable that there would be a surge of incidents requiring a response and thus arose the urgent need for an official mountain rescue team. Money was raised so that essential equipment could be purchased and an immediate call-out list of twenty men was drawn up, along with an additional pool of others on stand-by, who could be contacted at short notice. It was difficult to get in touch with the men in those days because there were no walkie-talkies, but all the more so in the absence of telephones in many houses, which meant that the only way to contact a member was often for a policeman to drive to his house. Assembling the men at night was particularly problematic: Alistair McCook, a founder member of the team, who lived in Nethybridge, recalls being regularly woken up by the police throwing stones at the slates beside his bedroom window. If the local cinema was operating, the police could save valuable time by storming in and shouting for those on the list, for with so few films shown, two or three of them were sure to be there. The rescuers then had to pick up their equipment, some of which was fairly primitive. They were not provided with head-lamps, but instead had to lug cumbersome lanterns, which required a 14-lb gas canister, and were similar to Tilley lamps.

Though new, upgraded equipment was continually purchased, it also became apparent that the team itself should be strengthened. This had been considered long before the Cairngorm Disaster of 1971, which I remember well, because that was the year we moved to Glentruim. Nobody who lived in the area at that time will ever forget it, nor the outcome of the Fatal Accident Inquiry at Banff, which was conducted the following year to scrutinise every aspect of the case.

One Friday afternoon, a group of two adults and fourteen children aged between fifteen and sixteen, from the mountaineering club of a school in Edinburgh, drove up to the outdoor centre at Lagganlia, near Feshie Bridge. They planned to make for the summit of Ben Macdhui early the next morning. The young man in charge was an outdoor activities leader, a competent and experienced instructor, and his female colleague, similarly well-regarded, was a third-year student of physical education in Fife. On the Saturday morning the group was divided into two. Eight of the fitter and more experienced children went with the male instructor, while the young woman took the relative novices, accompanied by an eighteen-year-old girl, a student teacher who was hoping to become a voluntary instructor at Lagganlia.

Their intention was to cross the Cairngorm plateau that first day, meeting up at the Corrour Bothy in the evening. The young woman had arranged to take her group from there on through the Lairig Ghru, whereas the male leader planned a more demanding route for his party, but both hoped their eventual rendezvous would be at Loch Morlich. By way of a contingency plan, they also decided that should the weather turn stormy on the Saturday, they would head for the Curran Bothy near Lochan Buidhe, instead of the Corrour Bothy.

The larger, more experienced party set out first, but by the time they reached the summit of Cairngorm the weather had already deteriorated. Since they were well-equipped, they continued, but, given the conditions, altered their route to one that was less arduous. They were knee-deep in unconsolidated powder snow and, according to the subsequent report, 'a strengthening wind veering to the south-east was soon driving snow straight into the children's faces'. After a struggle for three long miles in difficult conditions, the party reached the shelter of the Curran Bothy, the floor-space of which was only eight by twelve feet, very cramped for nine people.

In the meantime, the party of six children and two women was experiencing extreme difficulty, struggling to wade through the snow, which was falling heavily. The blizzard conditions worsened. Some of the young girls began to cry with exhaustion and fear, but it had become far too treacherous to go on, yet impossible to turn back. With no hope of reaching the bothy, their leader decided that they should make a shelter in the snow. However, this proved impractical because it was too soft, so they did the only thing they could, which was to build a semicircular wall of snow, behind which they sheltered in their sleeping-bags and plastic bivvy-bags. The weather was relentless and though the leader frequently got up to clear the snow off the children to prevent them from being buried, her efforts proved increasingly fruitless. The following morning, which was Sunday, she tried to go for help with one of the boys, but they were forced back by a vicious blizzard. By this time, another of the boys was completely buried under the snow and two of the girls had to be given an equipment bag to cram into, having lost their sleeping-bags.

The group of nine was lucky to return safely, particularly having experienced a hazardous descent into the Lairig Ghru. The alarm was raised for the second group and three search parties, each including two instructors, went out into the blizzards, but alas were forced back by the treacherous conditions. It was only on the Monday morning that the leader of the lost party was spotted by a Glenmore Lodge instructor aboard an RAF helicopter as she was crawling through the snow towards Glenmore. When rescued, she was able to speak only three words, which indicated the position of the children, then was immediately taken to hospital suffering from exposure and frostbite.

The rescue team found the children in the late afternoon. Only one boy out of the seven had survived, because, although buried beneath the snow, he had an air-pocket around his head. He was taken by helicopter to Inverness. Unfortunately, because of the deteriorating weather, the bodies of the other children had to be left where they were until the following day.

At the enquiry the following year, there was a discussion regarding the use of certain bothies high up in the Cairngorms. It was thought that they gave a false sense of security to inexperienced walkers, who might feel that no matter how bad the weather, there would be somewhere safe to shelter nearby. I believe that some of these shelters were later removed.

In January 1972 the local chief inspector of police placed an advertisement in the local newspaper, hoping to attract people willing to join the mountain rescue team. Nearly seventy individuals expressed interest, of whom thirty-six were engaged, all of them aware of the importance of a strong team spirit. John Allen, a pharmacist in Kingussie, was among those recruited; he became a team-leader, and later chairman of the organisation, receiving an MBE for his work.

With over thirty-four years of experience in the Cairngorm Mountain Rescue Team, John could fill volumes recounting the incidents he attended. The call-outs were not always for accidents on the mountains, but also entailed searches for missing persons in the valley, suicide attempts and people trapped in cars. Rock-climbing has also always had its share of incidents, some more serious than others, but it was good to hear some of the success stories. He told me about a couple of men who were carrying out an ice-climb on Coire an t-Sneachda when their rope got jammed. The lead climber, unable to pull his partner up, became frightened, untied his end of the rope and left his mate dangling. Fortunately, the shouts of the abandoned climber were heard by other people on the mountain and a 999 call was made. He was lucky to be rescued and his friend, found walking aimlessly across the plateau at the top of the climb, was also brought safely home.

John related another, more recent, incident that had a lot of media attention. A teacher led thirty-eight children up the same mountain without a map, compass or adequate clothing. The group was originally from a party of sixty, all of whom were staying at Nethy House, but because it had started to rain that morning, twenty-one of them, including three teachers, had turned back. The incompetent organisation of this expedition shocked the whole of Badenoch and Strathspey. Later, just before

138

5 p.m., the teacher made a 999 call on her mobile phone from somewhere on Meall a Bhuachaille, which is 2,500 ft high.

Alerted by the police, John phoned Tim Walker, the warden of Glenmore Lodge, who was at his home in Boat of Garten, to ask if he knew of a group that had gone up into the hills that day. As they spoke, Tim trained his binoculars towards the mountain and saw figures scattered beneath the low clouds, and indeed, the party was not far from safety. John rang the teacher on her mobile, but when she answered he could hear children screaming in the background. An experienced hillwalker would have had a map and compass, as well as the capacity to follow instructions, but this party had no such advantage. John tried his best to talk the teacher down from the mountain, which should have been an easy matter because the low clouds were moving. Though the group would soon have been in the clear, the teacher refused to be guided by telephone and demanded to be rescued.

The group consisted of girls from London, aged between sixteen and eighteen. They had ignored all advice that morning, which emphasised the danger of the hills in such weather. In addition, they had set off knowing nothing about the mountains and were inappropriately dressed for the prevailing conditions. The girls were wearing knee-length grey school skirts, black tights or socks, cardigans or fleeces, and trainers. On reaching the summit, the mist came down, winds blew up and the rain swept across the mountain range. They soon became disorientated and lost their way. Ironically, the teacher had first used her mobile to ask their bus driver to come up the hill for them, just as though ordering a taxi in London! Later, when she realised how serious the situation was, she even had the audacity to request a helicopter. It took the rescue team three hours to get them all safely down. The girls were found scattered across the mountainside and, according to John, some were exhausted, shivering and panicking, whilst others treated the rescue as a 'big joke'. The girls who made the flippant remarks were apparently less than polite and even grumbled about the time it took the rescue team to reach them! 'Where have you been?' and 'What kept you?' they were heard to say. One of the rescuers replied, 'Listen, I have given up my evening meal to come and rescue you!'

The girls all trooped down, followed by the teacher, who was under the impression that she had done no wrong. John put forward his hand, a gesture he was in the habit of making, as a welcome and an introduction, but the teacher withheld hers, saying, 'I do not shake hands with men.' He was taken aback by her action, and was only placated by the thought that such coolness was something to do with her religion. The teacher and girls were questioned about maps and compasses, but were quick to blame others for their lack of the most basic equipment. Even if they had possessed these items, they would certainly not have known how to use them. Land Rovers had been organised to take the school party back to their bus, but because they had been so unappreciative and rude, they were all left to walk back, apart from those who were too exhausted or had injuries, such as sprains!

When newspaper reporters arrived on the scene, John, as leader of the rescue team, told them how appalled he and his colleagues had been to discover that the girls were wearing inadequate clothing, with only bin-liners and plastic sheets wrapped round them as waterproofs. He added that it was one of the worst cases of lack of preparation on the part of a school group leader that he had ever encountered. The Cairngorm Mountain Rescue Team had been called out on a mission that could easily have been avoided had the school insisted on adequate expertise and planning. On the contrary, it was obvious that the party had not realised how dangerous a situation they had got themselves into or how near to tragedy they were. The teacher had put the girls' lives at risk by 'breaking every rule in the book', as John put it. Only the previous week, two fourteen-year-old boys had suffered hypothermia at a lower altitude in the same mountains.

There is, however, an amusing tale of a man who was reported missing by his wife one winter's night. Once alerted, the rescue team asked her to tell them as much as she could about his intended route and made their way up the ski-piste from the bottom car park. They had not been trekking through the snow for long when one of the team thought he heard shouts. Then further calls were heard, which, curiously, seemed to come from on high! 'He's up in the air', a member of the team cried, pointing up to a stationary chairlift. There he was, swinging in one of the chairs!

The lifts had been put out of action while engineers carried out repairs, during which the machinery had to be started and stopped at different intervals. Their day's work done, the engineers had gone home. Coming down the mountain cold and tired, the man had seen a moving chairlift and decided to catch a ride for the last part of his journey. At its upper terminal was a platform, from which he had managed to jump on board, but had not realised that the chair was only to move a fraction before the engineers knocked off for the night. So there he was, stranded. Although there was a net below the platform itself, the chair had unfortunately stopped just past it. He decided that it might be possible to jump onto the snow below, so he threw down his gear to ascertain the drop. It was too far, he reckoned, which meant he was marooned, cold and hungry, deprived of his head-light, gloves, food, drink and any other comforts, all of which were in his rucksack. He had been there for hours, frozen, before the rescue team rigged a wire from the platform to the chair and brought him down.

Despite the potential hazards, people love the hills for many reasons and it is good to see them enjoying their chosen sports. Even bitter cold rarely deters true enthusiasts from climbing, walking or skiing. One individual, however, must have found it colder than others, for still available in the local shops is a comical postcard bearing the image of a man skiing down the slopes, wearing not a stitch of clothing. Paulow Satney, the photographer whom we commissioned to record our daughter's wedding, was approached by a character from Glasgow who offered to pose naked while skiing downhill. The idea was to give Paulow a sensational shot. Paul, as he is better known, accepted the offer.

It was quite a risky operation, because once the volunteer had stripped at the top of the piste, he had to be sure that there was a reliable person to carry his clothes down to the car park. Paul smiled as he recalled that day. 'It was really very funny watching the faces of those who were sitting having lunch at the Ptarmigan,' he said. 'You could see heads turn in disbelief when suddenly the apparition of a naked skier swooped past. No one would have dreamt that anybody could be so foolish as to take off their clothes in the freezing snow, particularly at the perishing cold summit.' The photographs were taken, after which posters and postcards were produced, all for the open market. The pictures were even shown on a Terry Wogan television programme. The whole exercise was a great hit! According to the Cairngorm Mountain Rescue Team, hypothermia is one of the greatest dangers people face when lost in the mountains, but luckily this skier knew where he was going.

The Cairngorm Mountain Rescue Team still continues with its invaluable work, reliable whatever the nature of the demands made upon it. Innumerable people who might otherwise have perished owe their lives to its courageous, steadfast members, whose knowledge of the area they serve and diverse skills must never be taken for granted.

15

The Herd-Boy

IN the 1890s, many young men left Badenoch and Strathspey to seek their fortunes, some emigrating to Australia or New Zealand, as did one George Macpherson, better known as Geordie. His parents, both members of the Clan Macpherson, met while they were in service at Cluny Castle, married and subsequently had eleven children. Geordie was born in Laggan in 1885, but his family later moved to Luib, on the banks of the Calder.

In extreme old age, Geordie described his life in the Highlands as 'meagre, hard and restricted'. As a boy he would listen to the young men, home on leave, as they talked about their future in exciting and exotic places far, far away. Like others of his age, he was eager to explore those intriguing new countries in pursuit of adventure and opportunity himself.

Georgie recalled that it was usual for boys, when they were about eleven years old, to go herding during the six-week summer holidays. They would be employed by the crofters and part of their job was to take the cows across to the Dell. This grazing lay mainly in the fields of Newtonmore, between the River Spey and the railway line, and once the cows had been herded there it was the responsibility of the boys to look after them for the day. It was not too difficult for them to occupy themselves as the cows chewed away at the grass: swimming in the river, running along its banks and looking for birds' nests were often their sources of amusement. Geordie's career in fact began at the early age of nine, when a crofter engaged him for the whole summer holiday for six threepenny bits, a wage of which he was very proud. On payday, the wife of the crofter put his money into an envelope, then carefully stitched it into the inside pocket of his jacket before he left. Geordie thought that the crofter's wife must have been safeguarding him from highway men, for his earnings were indeed a princely sum in those days. By the time he was twelve, he had graduated to what he called the 'big world of herd-boys' and now considered himself something of a professional. His job prevented him from going to school for six months of the year, which meant that he had to catch up with his studies during the remaining months, not always an easy task.

Most of the villagers had a single cow per household. As part of the daily routine, one of a group of about six herd-boys would collect each beast, leading it from its owner's home to join the others, so that by the time the cows reached the Dell, the herd was complete. Each boy would then take charge of three to five cows. One cow in particular apparently required no prompting at all first thing in the morning, for she always came out and joined the herd on hearing the sound of a horn played by one of the boys.

During hot spells the boys would often be in the river, swimming and playing games. A favourite pastime was to float downstream to the edge of the rapids, then quickly jump out and run back to start all over again. They would keep going until they were exhausted and, needless to say, always swam in their 'birthday suits'! As with all young boys, there were dares and dangerous pranks, and one of the lads nearly came to grief while showing off. The others suddenly realised that he was missing, but luckily they noticed two feet sticking up out of the water. They dived in and pulled their friend out of the pool by his feet and, even with no first-aid training, managed to resuscitate him.

144

While they were pumping out the water, they noticed bruises on either side of his head and wondered what had caused them. On investigation, the boys discovered two large boulders close together in the water and, because of the extraordinary position they had found their friend in, assumed that his head must have been jammed between them!

Every year a cow was slaughtered to give to the poor and the sick, and Geordie admitted to having been involved in a very childish trick just as the deed was about to be done. The killing was to be just before nightfall, in the usual place outside the village. He and his friends had decided to take an egg each and throw it at the wall behind the cow at the moment it was slaughtered. It was a solemn exercise by the sounds of it, with a ceremony as sombre as that performed by a high priest. As dusk fell, about seven men were huddled together, studiously watching by the dim light of a lantern the stunning instrument poised for action, when one of the boys prematurely threw an egg. It hit the 'high priest' on the forehead and the contents started to drip down his face. For some reason the man thought he had hit himself with the weapon he was holding in his hand and presumed that it was blood trickling down his cheek. 'I'm killed, I'm killed. My brains are running out,' he shouted. The other men soon found out that it was egg they were wiping off their friend's face, not brains! The chase for the culprit began and the cow was left bewildered, but unharmed.

The disadvantage of missing school for such long periods each year was undoubtedly to blame for their lack of knowledge, but their teacher unfortunately made much of this fact and indeed used it as an outlet for his sadistic and sarcastic nature. He ridiculed them in front of the whole class and referred to them as 'cows' tails'. It was understandable that they would be behind in their work, but to make a joke of it was unkind and unprofessional.

This schoolmaster took special delight in mocking anyone with a disability or deformity. A youngster with a bad stutter in the same class as Geordie was picked on in front of everyone because of his impairment. Instead of helping him correct it or trying to give him confidence, the teacher would do just the reverse by mimicking him to make the other pupils laugh. Another child had a head-shake, which gave him a further victim on whom to vent his spleen. This particular pupil accepted his humiliation until he could bear it no longer. He threw his unframed slate at his persecutor; it missed him, but its sharp edge pierced the wall behind. Had it not missed, it could have caused a nasty wound. The boy then headed off, straight for home. Shortly after this scene, his father, described as a large hairy man with a voice like thunder, burst into the classroom and a chase round the table ensued. Those who wore kilts to school were also subject to the master's scorn, among them three brothers who were bullied so badly that their parents took them away from Newtonmore and sent them to Kingussie instead. A three-mile walk each day was preferable to abuse from the schoolmaster.

Occasionally there was other work available, supplementing the herd-boys' seasonal wages from working in the Dell. Geordie managed to secure a few such jobs, including one which entailed mucking out a donkey's shed for a crippled old man who could no longer do it himself. The shed had always been mucked out once a year 'whether it needed it or not' and Geordie could see straight away what was required, for the shed was so full of dung that the door could scarcely be opened. Once the work was completed, he was proud of his achievement and there was even room for another donkey! He earned a half-penny for his pains.

Donkeys were used to pull the carts which carried barrels of herrings, creating yet another occupation by which the young could earn easy money. They would shout 'Fresh herrings!' as they went through the villages and passed potential customers' doors. The crippled man who sold the herrings was commonly known as 'the cripple man who sells herring'! It is interesting to note that people were often named after their work or afflictions, with no offence or stigma attached. It was merely a way of instant identification.

Fresh herrings were also sold by the tinkers who travelled through the valley. 'Fresh herrings, three for a penny', they shouted out as they passed with their barrels. It seems they considered it important to call out the price, for all the housewives wished to know how much they might have to spend before they went out into the street. The herrings were large and made a 'goodly' family meal, especially when cooked on top of potatoes.

News of work opportunities often came by word of mouth. Geordie was once approached by a builder to assist with the construction of a new hotel. He was delighted at this proposition, but the builder suggested that he should ask his parents first. Although Geordie did not think their consent necessary, he did as he was told – to his cost. His parents disagreed, for he had already been promised to the shoemaker! 'Alas! Alas!' Geordie retorted, 'my heart fell into my boots and I carried it there for days, first in one boot then in the other.'

The job of a shoemaker's apprentice was not at all like working in the fields, so Geordie's spirit was dampened, always longing for the wilds again. He also wondered why the place he worked in was called a shoemaker's shop, for it was all boots that he was dealing with. 'Boots, boots, boots! Large and small, from the smallest child's to the largest man's, heavy hob-nailed farm boots, all made by hand.' Jokes were always played on the new apprentice, just as they would have been on any new boy at school. Not long after he started work with the shoemaker, he was sent on an errand to the local store. For this assignment he was given a wee tin and told to bring back a pennyworth of pigeon-milk. He duly went to the shopkeeper, who smiled and gave him a caraway-seed biscuit to go back with!

This was not the ideal workplace for Geordie, who kept thinking of the open spaces and the time when he worked alongside his father at Luib. The boot workshop was stuffy and smelly, while the hills and the countryside were clean and fresh. At weekends, pleased to be outdoors again, he watched his father train their horses for the water-wheel, each horse being attached to a long pole and going round and round. Once the mill had started up, the big building would be filled with a rumbling sound and shake with the machinery's vibration. Sheaves would be fed into the machine, after which would come the rushing, whispering sound of grain down the chute. When the chaff had slid softly down and filled the containers beneath, Geordie was expected to empty them. Because it seemed such a responsible task for a small boy, Geordie felt like a king.

Strangely, it was the work in the cold weather that he loved most. How he enjoyed the wintry weather, when the heat and steam from the animals made the byre feel like a hot-house! The byres were divided up so that each cow had a stall, as did the horses in their stables. Manure from these sheds was barrowed out to the yard, where it was allowed to rot before being thrown over the potato drills. It was satisfying work indeed.

Sometimes the herd-boys helped themselves to little freshly dug potatoes that the diggers had missed. They would boil them up in an old tin can over an open fire somewhere out on the hill or down in the pasture below. The wee tatties tasted far better out there, cooked in this crude fashion, than in the pot at home. For the same reason, Angie always used to say that tea brewed outdoors was preferable to any other. A herd-boy's dog might sniff out a hare which had unwittingly popped its head through a hole in the wall and would then chase it flat-out, and, with any luck, catch it. It would be gutted, with its skin left intact, and cooked outside. It too would be delicious.

In those days, the grouse season brought numerous visitors to the villages and several of the larger houses were let, some with staff. As well as the sport, tourists came to drink from Highland springs and, above all, to breathe clean, fresh air, a little of which they hoped to retain in their lungs when they returned to the smog and smoke of their homes in the cities. Since beaters were required for shoots on local estates, many of the young lads would be hired and out they would go, beating the heather to make the birds rise. Some would also have poles with flags attached; when only grouse flew over, they would shake their flags and send the birds in the direction of the butts, where guns were prepared and ready to fire. The beaters were proud of the way they carried out their duties and felt responsible for the number of birds in the bags at the end of the day; if they were given a mention for their efforts, they were even more delighted. Geordie was informed one day, by a friend in the know, that if, following a break, positions were changed for those more favourable, it could mean that there had been 'a little bribery per the whisky bottle'.

Driving was not easy then for the beaters, for there were no vehicles to take them to their stations. They might have to walk seven miles, but one pound in wages for the week was superior to three shillings and sixpence for being an apprentice, Geordie thought. He gave his earnings to his mother, of which sixpence was handed back. Little wonder his mother was eager to keep some of this income, for three pounds would have bought her a three-piece suite in those days.

In summer, 4 June used to be a holiday in Scotland, a fast day, but not universally observed. Nevertheless, it was a chance for a whole day's fishing, which was considered a leisurely pastime. Indeed, it was a major part of the way of life of country people. It was bred into them, as in every one of their forebears – all the local boys were 'daft' on fishing. Geordie wrote about grabbing opportunities 'between the two lights', the rough translation of a Gaelic expression meaning the time of day when it was not quite light enough to read or carry out chores, not yet dark enough to stop work for the evening, in other words the gloaming. It was only then that fish were said to 'rise gallantly' and thus the ideal time to go down to the pools to catch them.

149

I remember my own precious hours 'between the two lights' at Glentruim, before the long, dark evenings. It was the hour to put a match to the fire after a cold, exhausting day, knowing that soon I would be able to sit down and relax in warmth for the remaining hours before bed. For me this was almost a ritual, a reward for working hard, a part of the day I longed for. There was nothing nicer or more relaxing than watching the flames dance in the fire, listening to the crackle of burning twigs as they sparked in the glowing cinders. Thinking back, I suspect that this is why I love the long dark nights of winter, unlike anyone else I know. I could easily understand Geordie's translation: there is no need for an English word.

In Geordie's day, the local doctor had to be a man broadly skilled in every aspect of his profession. As a boy, Geordie recalled seeing his GP on two occasions, the first when he was whacked by a shinty stick, which caused severe bruising, and the second when he had to have a tooth out, for there were no local dentists at that time. The doctor pulled the wrong one with his crude pliers and, having apologised profusely, offered to try again, but Geordie gracefully declined, saying 'No thanks, I couldn't stand it.' He noted that there was a visible trail of blood all the way from Kingussie to Newtonmore that day!

Although there was a lack of dental professionals, there were many other excellent facilities for those who lived in the area, even in Geordie's parent's day. In Laggan alone there were six shops with every kind of commodity one could ask for, 'from wool to anchors', as Angus Macpherson (son of the famous piper, Malcom) noted. Apart from shops selling household provisions, there were tailors, kilt-makers, boot-makers and even two well-run hotels. However, as there was no dentist, Angus once found himself carrying out emergency treatment in this field.

He had been busy with his house-letting agency when an elderly local came into his office with raging toothache. He had asked both the joiner and the shoemaker to extract his tooth for him, but they

150

had refused. He then asked Angus the same favour, in his best Gaelic, and added that the shoemaker had kindly lent him a pair of pliers suitable for the job. Angus was naturally reluctant, but nevertheless took the patient into his back room and sat him down. All the teeth looked as if they should be pulled, but Angus acquired a good hold and in less than two seconds the offending tooth was on the floor. At least that old man's rotten tooth was removed, which was more than could be said for poor Geordie!

Wandering the hills and dells where the wildlife ran freely, scanning the ridges for birds of prey, was all part of a herd-boy's day. One of Geordie's favourite places was the burn which ran down to the farm below the plateau. 'It fell over the cliff and gave the most delightful spray,' wrote Geordie. There was a large black rock, half in and half out of the water, where young eels would slither across and bask in the sun, and the spray would keep them moist, so that they could spend hours hardly moving. The seclusion of this special place made Geordie feel that it belonged to him alone and he felt protective of his solitude.

The herd-boys were tough, but not 'roughies', and were from decent, respectable families. Even though they did not always manage to attend church on the Sabbath, as was compulsory in those days, they were nevertheless Christians and would go out of their way to carry out a good turn. They were all brought up to respect their elders and their parents, 'even if it wasn't always apparent', Geordie wrote. Whatever the rigours, their outdoor working lives were enjoyable as well as healthy, with fresh air and plenty of exercise, which allowed them to build up their muscles and develop their sporting skills. Few of those youngsters ever experienced such carefree days again in their lives.

When Geordie Macpheron documented his memoirs in 1982, he was ninety-seven years old. He had started his days in Laggan, at a time when jobs were becoming scarce, though in the previous century work had been plentiful there. For that reason, he was obliged to move to Newtonmore and then much further afield to seek work. He eventually settled in New Zealand, where he died at the age of 104 in 1990. Perhaps he owed his longevity to his hardy, yet carefree upbringing in Newtonmore. For him and for a great many others who were obliged to travel abroad to find work, their ties with home were never broken, for in their minds they always held fast to their native land.

After Geordie died, his wife wrote a poem in his memory which summed up nostalgic moments, and sent it back to Newtonmore.

[Rare White Heather]
Sprigs of heather now remind me of my youth in Newtonmore
Where as lads we'd climb together gentle slopes of craig an
    Laun,
Seeking for the rare white heather nestling in a secret covey
In the Glen of Banchor.

Why it was so precious to us, at the time we did not know
Now like jewels of ancient wisdom memories pierce the
    sacred lore
And we breathe the heavenly perfume
Found only in the Glen of Banchor.

As Scot in this far homeland and the oceans now divide us
    I recall
The days of seeking, not a thought about the weather,
Just the scent of native heather,
Droning bees and startled birds all combine to give a picture
Of the Glen of Banchor.

If you were a Highland lad away from school on holiday,
You'd go seeking rare white heather where it grew one other
    summer

On gentle slopes, a secret place above the River Calder criss
    and crossing o'er the vale
Of the lovely Glen of Banchor.

16

Amongst the Heather

ONE of the glories of Scotland is the bracken and heather that flourish across its hills, their soft colours especially beautiful in late summer and early autumn, when russet is splashed with different shades of purple. The moors above Glentruim have always been as thickly covered by them as anywhere else in the Highlands, and, during the summers of the years we lived there, we would walk for miles enjoying the splendour that surrounded us, ever watchful for the odd sprig of 'lucky' white heather to pick and take home. Heather is a plant for all occasions, and we often used it for arrangements in the house, either in little vases or else in old, hand-painted, washstand basins, as used in the days before modern plumbing. The annual regeneration of heather is important to wildlife, for creatures that roam the hills depend on its nutritious properties. It should be well-managed and conserved, not only for its intrinsic beauty, but also for the preservation of game, which, of course, is essential to the viability of sporting estates.

Heather-burning is usually carried out between October and the middle of the following April, and during these months plumes of smoke can be observed above the horizon, gently billowing up into the sky. As a matter of routine our gamekeeper, accompanied by Euan, would diligently take to the hills every year for this specific purpose. The heather would be burned in strips, and the men would not come home until they knew that it was safe to leave. If, however, following a hot spell of weather, the heather was bone-dry, extreme care had to be taken, for the flames could run away within seconds, speeding out of control for miles.

In 1972, the year after we arrived at Glentruim, David and Betty Lambie opened the Scottish Heather Centre in Skye of Curr. They came from Lanarkshire, but had fallen in love with Speyside many years before, on their honeymoon. Through sheer determination and relentless hard work, their renowned business has grown, bringing them trade from all over the world. The saying 'From small acorns large oak trees grow' has certainly been true for the Lambies. They started by selling heather from a shed on a small plot of land, where they also built an outdoor picnic area. During the winter, however, they made use of a large cupboard inside their make-shift shop for serving tea and shortbread. A table and four chairs could only just fit into this space. 'It must have been the smallest tea-room in the world!' Betty said. Today they have built up a huge enterprise, incorporating gardens, shops, exhibitions and a restaurant.

David first found his passion for different varieties of heather when he was working at the Royal Horticultural Society's garden at Wisley, and Betty, also interested in plants and flowers, trained as a florist in Glasgow and London, later running her own shops. Well-travelled, they each gleaned extensive knowledge and skills in the field of horticulture, and eventually decided to combine their talents and start a business in the place to which they had longed to return.

In the course of investigating job-prospects and looking for somewhere to live, the opportunity arose for a partnership with a local general contractor called Sandy Grant at Skye of Curr, and thus David became involved in contract landscaping. Their new life began in a caravan on a corner-piece of ground adjacent to Sandy's house. At that particular time, Sandy had been negotiating purchase of this plot of land and, amazingly, offered a half-share to the Lambies, which they happily accepted. 'It was like Steptoe's yard, with old cars and junk all over the place,' David admitted. The caravan cost £1,000, of which £100 was paid immediately and the remainder settled within three years. Although it was a struggle, particularly as their children were only two and four years old at the time, they quickly got the business up and running.

Seeing their large development today, it is hard to believe that the Lambies started with only an old garage in the centre of a 'Steptoe's yard'. Originally they had heathers for sale in rows on the ground in front of the caravan, but later the pots were raised onto trestles, making them more eye-catching for buyers and thus encouraging more sales.

The shortbread for 'the smallest tea room in the world' was made by Betty in their cramped caravan. She put up a sign at the end of the road to advertise "Tea and Home-baking which meant that she often had to stay up all night baking to guarantee supplies. Her family were given strict instructions never to eat the whole pieces, only the broken bits. This reminded me of all the cooking I used to do myself before the Clan Gathering every August, when we sometimes had over a hundred Macphersons to tea on the lawns at Glentruim. My family was given similar orders about shortbread: I knew how Betty felt!

Betty laughed as she told me how the shortbread once nearly caused a divorce. She had been working long and hard, looking after the children, making meals, selling heather and then baking into the early hours of the morning. By the time David came home from his landscaping work the next afternoon, she was overwhelmed with so many chores and totally exhausted. She happened to see him eating two perfect, whole pieces of short-bread and pounced on him.

'Is that you eating the perfect shortbread?' she demanded with some emotion.

'Stuff your bloody shortbread!' David shouted, hurling the half-eaten piece back at her, for he too was tired, and riled.

'Can you imagine what the judge would have said,' laughed Betty, 'when I explained that it was all because of the shortbread, M'Lord?'

There was more to Betty's achievements than excellent cooking, for she told me that she was also a trained chiropodist. I found it comical to think that one minute she was pressing shortbread into tins and the next paring down a foot! To survive, all skills had to be used to keep food on the table, just as I had discovered at Glentruim, whether I liked it or not.

The chiropody qualification gave Betty the means bring in extra income. She recalled an unsavoury incident when an 'old worthy', as she described him, had come to the caravan one day for an appointment. Having taken off his wellie boots, his feet were so filthy that it looked as if he had not washed them for weeks. Betty said the smell was overpowering, but she did not have the guts to tell him to go and wash them.

'If you go home and soak your feet, it would make it easier for me, because then the skin will be softer,' she said tactfully, thinking that this was a strong enough hint to encourage him to give his feet a good scrub. But no, he came back later and declared, "I just put the wellies back on and let my feet have a good sweat!"

'My nose is nearer than yours,' remarked Betty tartly, as she tried yet again to persuade him to go home and wash his feet.

In their caravan days, the Lambies took on every job they could possibly manage, including one in particular that was too good to miss. A PR company from London had been asked to decorate the Coylumbridge ice-rink for a seasonal function, but because they had been let down by their usual contractor, they urgently needed another company to take on the assignment. It was a dreich November's day when the call came from the PR representative, a lady with a very 'hoity-toity' voice, I was told. Betty, in desperation for the contract, put on her best English accent and informed this agent that her husband was an experienced landscape designer and would be happy to take on the work, which included the provision of a number of six-foot trees and some half-barrels by 6 p.m. While engaged in conversation, Betty was looking out of the window at the trees in their garden, thinking, 'They're ready for chopping; needs must when the family has to be fed!'

As soon as David and his young lad arrived back at the caravan later that afternoon, Betty told them about the contract she had accepted, and so, directly after their tea, the men felled the trees and loaded them along with the barrels into the old lorry. In the meantime, Betty dressed up in her smartest clothes and drove over to Coylumbridge. David, however, had no time to change and was still wearing his old jacket tied with string, wellies and a knitted hat as he followed her in his lorry. His attire had bothered him not a bit, having previously spent most of his days in a white collar and tie; he enjoyed the extreme contrast of being a country bumpkin and looking like a tramp!

As arranged, Betty met the lady from London at the hotel, engaging her in polite conversation to buy time until the men arrived. She then escorted her out to the car park, where they found David and his assistant striding towards them, both tired but smiling broadly. Betty cringed as she looked at her scruffy, grubby husband, thinking, 'I cannot possibly introduce him as the professional landscaper!'

'These are the lads,' said Betty brightly, glancing at David, her eyes defying him to give the game away as she introduced them to their client.

'Yes, Mrs Lambie,' David replied after each of the questions she put to him. 'Three bags full, Mrs Lambie,' he thought, with a grin on his face. He had actually been disowned by his wife for a brief moment, though they laughed about it later.

The business started to expand, and having at last purchased their plot of land, the Lambies were able to plan a new tea-room. For this, the old School House at Rothiemurcus was bought, split into sections and re-erected where the old potting shed had stood. In addition, site-huts formerly used on the old A9 also were utilised as dividers in their new shop. The place was transformed and attracted even more visitors.

The new tearoom was called The Original Clootie Dumpling Restaurant, its speciality, of course, being clootie dumpling, a traditional sweet pudding steamed in a muslin cloth. The Lambies have managed to devise over twenty-two ways of serving the dumpling, their recipes involving ingredients such as chocolate, ice-cream, liqueurs and fruit, among other things. All very tempting and delicious. I have noticed that when local people talk about the Heather Centre, they very often refer to it as 'The Clootie Dumpling', which proves the Lambie's success: their proof is in their pudding!

Everything at the centre is of a high quality, and its permanent exhibition is most informative on the subject of varieties of heather, as well as describing its diverse uses in the past and the present. I was intrigued to learn that heather was used not only to make brooms, walking sticks and chimney brushes, but also baskets, mats and ropes. Indeed, woven ropes of heather decorate the Royal Pavilion at the Braemar Games each year. The plant had also been worn in the past as camouflage, for deer-stalking, and bridal head-dresses have even been made from heather. What is more unusual still is the process by which heather can be made into floor-tiles, for when compressed, it produces a firm, solid surface; the same method is used for the colourful jewellery sold in the craft shop.

The Scottish Heather Centre at Skye of Curr is now a great tourist attraction, a bonus for the whole of Speyside. Perhaps the owners' passion for heather has given them the luck said to be associated with white heather. A tea-towel hanging on display in the shop bears the story of White Heather, which is this:

The Celtic bard Ossian had a beautiful daughter, Malvina,

who was as good as she was lovely. She was betrothed to Oscar, bravest of all the warriors.

One fine autumn day, as Malvina listened to her father's music and thought of her beloved Oscar's imminent return from a war-like expedition, she saw a figure limping towards them over the heather-clad moor. It was Oscar's faithful messenger, who, wounded and weary, knelt before her, gave her a sprig of purple heather and told her that Oscar was slain in battle. As he lay dying, Oscar had plucked the heather and asked that it be given to Malvina as a token of his eternal love. As she listened, tears fell from Malvina's eyes onto the purple heather. It immediately became white!

Thereafter, as father and daughter walked over the moors, Malvina's tears fell upon patches of purple heather, turning them white. Even in the depths of her sadness, wishing that others might be happier than she, Malvina prayed thus, 'May the White Heather, symbol of my sorrow, bring good fortune to all who find it.'

After the Annual General Meeting during our Clan Gatherings, a basket of white heather is passed around, so that each member has a sprig to wear at the Clan March and for the rest of the weekend. Superstition or not, all gladly honour this tradition of the Macpherson Clan, which is one of the largest in the world, close and thriving. We are lucky to be members, and perhaps the white heather serves as a small reminder of our strong fellowship.

17

Highland Spirits

A supernatural being called a kelpie, a malevolent water-spirit, is reputed to haunt Loch Pityoulish, which is at the other end of the valley from Laggan. Though kelpies generally appear in the form of horses, they are also able to transform themselves to appear as attractive young men or women. Their aim is to entice people into the water to drown them. It is said that kelpies wear magnificent bridles with magical powers; if you were to look through the eyelets of these bridles, you would be able to see things usually invisible to the human eye. If you travel through Carrbridge on the old A9, passing under the railway bridge and across the moor, there is a viaduct just before Slocht, near which you will find a wee lochan where a kelpie was said to live.

There is an old story of a certain young Kincardine, who was enjoying a day out by the side of the loch with some of his friends when a beautiful black horse trotted along the banks towards them. When it reached the boys, it bowed its head as if to invite them to have a ride. Kincardine fondly stroked its mane while several of the others leapt onto its back, but as he did so, he realised that the creature was not a horse at all, but a kelpie. Suddenly it reared, Kincardine's hand stuck to its mane and his friends found themselves trapped on its back. The kelpie leapt into the loch, dragging the boys deeper and deeper into its dark, icy depths. As they all went down, Kincardine pulled out his dirk and cut off his fingers on the hand that was stuck to the kelpie. Once the painful deed was done, he swiftly rose to the surface, blood trailing behind him. The encounter with the kelpie left him without fingers on one hand, but he survived, which was a more fortunate fate than that of his friends.

Strange beings and even stranger happenings were not un-expected in the Highlands of the past. Willox McGregor, a warlock, lived upstream from Tomintoul in the eighteenth century and was a well-documented figure. Two objects gave him curative powers, one a bridle and the other a stone. A friend of mine, who knows a great deal about Strathspey and Badenoch, once told me that in the 1970s he was shown a charm stone in the parish of Abernethy, on condition that he never revealed its whereabouts. It turned out to be the famous stone of Willox, which was sitting on an ordinary card table outside a house! Old beliefs evidently live on.

Other lochs too had their strange phenomena. People claimed to have seen a 'carnivorous water monster' in Loch Garten, for example. This creature was described as 'a cross between a large bull and a stallion with jet black mane, big head, broad back and glaring eyes'. It was never seen by day, but was said to prey on children and lambs at night, when its roars could be heard throughout the valley. Whether children would have been anywhere near the loch and its burns at night is questionable; I suspect children would have been tucked up in their beds by then and if not, perhaps the threat of such a monster helped parents to persuade them to go to sleep at a reasonable hour!

In the 1990s Affleck Grey described the perils of the River Spey in stormy weather, regretting the number of lives this river had claimed: 'Little wonder that in older days the people who lived close to the Spey believed in an evil spirit that lurked in its depths.' He may be referring to kelpies, for when the water became high and wild, the imagination tended to take hold. Unlike other kelpies, which were usually black, those from the

Spey were white, except for those in deeper pools, which were allegedly yellow. The latter preyed on young girls and newlywed couples, luring them into the water and devouring them forthwith. Had one been brought up constantly hearing these fables and superstitions, it might have been easier to believe such fanciful explanations than think the obvious, that someone had drowned in turbulent waters.

People also used to talk about fairy dogs (an cu glas) which, according to the locals, were green. It has been suggested that the description of these creatures' colour is incorrect and that the Gaelic word 'glas' has been wrongly used since the Victorian era. Glas does mean 'green' or 'greenish-blue' when describing colours of vegetation, but for animals the translation should be grey, as used for a grey seal, a grey she-wolf, or indeed grey mist (ceo glas). Furthermore, according to both Highland and Irish Gaelic traditions, fairy dogs interbred with mortal hounds, in which case the magnificent, tall, predominantly grey Scottish deer-hounds and Irish wolf-hounds may very well be their descendents. The fairy dogs were not considered as dangerous as kelpies, but to be followed by one and hear it bark three times was supposed to be an omen of death. The only way to pre-empt mortality was to stone the barking dog.

Less threatening than the 'green' dogs was a fairy hound called Brodain. He belonged to a hunter, Calum Ban, who lived near Loch a'Bhrodain, which was named after his dog many years after its death. Calum was an expert in training dogs and one day a demon came to the door with a litter of puppies, asking him to train them for him. The demon said he would be back once they were a bit older and that, in exchange for his trouble, he could keep one. Calum was delighted when they turned out to be superb hunting dogs, fast, nimble and able to outrun any hare.

The day came when the demon returned for his dogs and while he was gathering them all together, Calum reminded him of his promise. The demon was enraged, for he did not want Calum to have a fairy dog as good as his own, and in his fury, picked up the smallest black dog of the litter, broke one of its hind legs and threw it back at him. The wounded dog would now never run as fast as his dogs, thought the demon, vanishing with the rest of the hounds. He was wrong: Calum secured a splint on the injured leg and nurtured the dog back to full health. Although this animal would always be lame, it could run faster than any other Calum knew of.

At about this time, a magnificent white fairy hind appeared in the valley. It had the reputation of running like the wind, faster than any creature on the earth, and Calum's dream was for Brodain to run even faster than her. One day when Calum was out hunting with his dog along the shores of Loch Laggan, stalking from Ben Alder to Loch Ericht, he crossed over the hills to Gaick and spotted the white fairy deer. Immediately he sent Brodain after her and eagerly watched as the dog closed in on her. At one stage, he thought his dog was gaining on the hind, but just as they were alongside each other, they both jumped into Loch a'Bhrodain. Some said that they plunged into the water, going down deeper and deeper together, while others believed that in the middle of the loch the dog caught the hind just before they both went under. They were never seen again.

Witches and their nefarious ways are another sinister element of the folklore of this particular area, as elsewhere. South of Kingussie there was a wood, once part of the ancient Caledonian Forest, where it was said that formerly a coven of witches would meet near Hallowe'en to gather toadstools. These crones travelled from all over the country in search of fungi of many varieties and colours, including the deadly scarlet ones with white spots, all of which were carefully preserved for use as poison or for love potions. The witches were particularly interested in the area of Kingussie, for the red toadstools were so plentiful there that they resembled masses of poppies in the fields. Residents

166

were wary of dark, moonless nights and usually avoided the wood at dusk, but a young boy out one night on an errand said he had seen the witches 'flighting in like grey geese'. He told everyone that they had come riding in on all sorts of steeds, cats, broomsticks, straw and ragwort stalks being the most popular forms of mount. Horses were regularly taken from the local people and after a night out with the witches, their owners would find them exhausted the next morning, their manes in hag-knots, which were what the witches used as stirrups. According to legend, if the witches had known that they had been seen by the boy while they were in flight, they would have cut out his tongue. He was fortunate not to have been spotted.

Tales of other notorious witches abound in Kingussie, to the north of which is an old burial mound known as the Witch's Hill, where the most infamous of them all, the Witch of Laggan (Bean a Lagain), was rumoured to carry out her wicked business. Although witches were more commonly known to appear as ravens, she would also take the shape of a wolf, cat or hen, then drift around in all weathers, terrifying the locals. Young mothers would have their babies baptised as soon as possible, in case she appeared as a cat and sucked the infant's breath away. I was always told that a cat should be kept away from a pram so that it would not sit on the baby's face and smother it. This would have stemmed from a fear of witches.

One night a hunter known in the valley as a persecutor of witches was caught in a violent storm after a day's hunting in the forest of Gaick. Seeking shelter, he entered an old bothy, taking his two faithful dogs with him, and inside he built up a good fire to keep them warm for the night. After a while, he heard at the door the sound of a cat, which was making such a noise that he decided to investigate. It was large and black, but looked forlorn and bedraggled, drenched by the torrential rain. The cat spoke and admitted to being a witch, but said that she wished to repent of all her misdeeds, if only he would be kind enough to let her in to dry by the fire. The hunter relented, feeling sorry for her, but his dogs raised their hackles and growled ferociously. Passing him a couple of hairs from her head, she asked him to tie up his dogs, because they were making her nervous. He took the hairs and tied them to the rafters above, but only pretended to secure the other ends to the dogs.

Crouching by the fire, the cat warmed herself and gradually, before the hunter's very eyes, she grew bigger and bigger, her shape slowly changing from a cat into someone he recognised as the Good Wife of Laggan, a friend of his wife. He suddenly realised that the apparition must in fact be the fearful Witch of Laggan. The dogs became jumpy, baring their teeth and growling at this notorious being, who cackled and shrieked, 'Fasten hair, fasten!' She assumed that her strands of hair had been firmly tied to the dogs and then secured to the rafters, so that they could not attack her, but she was wrong. The hairs tightened so strongly that the rafters cracked and with no ties holding them back, the dogs leapt on her. Their teeth dug into her breast and they clung to her, but they were doomed to die from the poison of the witch's body. She took off into the night in the form of a raven as the two faithful dogs expired in front of their distraught master.

After the storm eased, the hunter buried his dogs and returned home to his wife. She was not there at first but when she returned, he discovered that she had been at the home of the Good Wife of Laggan, who seemed to be on her death-bed. Her sick friend had been out all day cutting peat and had been drenched, causing her severe colic, his wife told him. The hunter had his dinner, then put on his coat to visit the Good Wife of Laggan. Pushing past the neighbours who were already mourning her imminent demise, he approached the dying woman and stripped her of her clothes. There were teeth-marks on her breast, where his dogs had clung on to her flesh. She was indeed the

Witch of Laggan. She wailed in horror, realising that she was about to die and would be taken by Satan to burn in hell. Admitting all of the atrocities that she had committed, she died in front of her astonished neighbours and friends, who had always thought of her as a pious, upright member of the community.

Just at that moment, two travellers happened to be walking along the road towards Badenoch, when they saw a woman, covered in blood, screaming as she ran past them towards Dalarossie kirkyard. A black dog followed close behind her, with a second also in pursuit. Further along the road a man in black on a black horse passed by and asked them if they had seen a woman running past, chased by two dogs. When they answered in the affirmative, he enquired whether they thought the dogs would catch up with the woman before she reached Dalarossie kirkyard. They replied that it was a possibility. The travellers were unnerved by their experience and hurried on towards Glenbanchor, where they heard the horseman return. As the horse and rider sped past, they noticed that the woman had been slung across the saddle, with one dog fixed to her breast, the other to her thigh.

The rider, believed to be Satan himself, had caught up with the woman just before she entered the kirkyard of Dalarossie. It was the spirit of the Witch of Laggan that he was after and he had to catch her before she reached the sanctuary of the churchyard. If a witch or her spirit were to enter a churchyard, she would be freed immediately from all her ties with Satan. Unfortunately for the spirit of the Witch of Laggan, she was overtaken by the Devil, to whom she had once sold her soul, and did not reach her goal of redemption.

There are numerous descriptions of the demise of the Witch of Laggan, most of which relate to the tale of the hunter. Most feature her appearance as a cat and the tying of the hair to the rafters of the hut, although one variation tells of her disguising herself as a big black hen that grew and grew in front of the hunter's eyes before taking the form of the Witch of Laggan.

Another tale of the Witch of Laggan concerns her sheep straying into the cornfields belonging to her neighbour at Tigh na Caim. When the sheep were discovered by the shepherd, he impounded them and demanded payment from the witch. The witch retaliated in a vindictive manner: the shepherd's cows fell sick and died, his barn burned down and a big, black, ferocious cat haunted the house. The situation was so disastrous that the shepherd's wife became very frightened and the family left the district.

The next occupier of the house was Donald Bane, who was determined to protect himself from the witch and her powers. He hung horseshoes on doors, tied bog-firs (fossilised pine cones) on his animals and spread rowan branches around the buildings, but none of these methods deterred her. She continued prowling and the black cat was again seen in the house and preying on the poultry in the yard. Eventually Donald could not put up with this evil creature any longer. He loaded his gun with a silver bullet and took a shot at it. The cat was wounded in one leg and, as predicted, the next time the Witch of Laggan was seen, she was lame in one leg! Following her death, her remains were burned and buried on a hill, which later became the site for a war memorial.

★★★

During the fierce winter of 1912, a legend arose about a peddler called Peter Chisholm, who used to travel around the Highlands in all weathers. He relied on the goodness of the Highland folk as he trudged from place to place through deep snow with his box of wares, all his worldly goods strapped securely to his shoulder. He was making his way to shelter in an old keeper's cottage when, as so often happens in the Highlands, the weather suddenly started to deteriorate. He was only about three miles from his destination when blinding snow slowed his pace and the raw chill gnawed at his bones. Numb and frozen, he soon succumbed to the intense cold and dropped to the ground. The old man was found the next day by a shepherd and his son, who together managed to drag his body to a nearby cottage. The boy was then sent off to get help. Much to the surprise of the locals, no money was found on Peter, neither in his clothes nor in his box. It was well-known that he had carried all his possessions around with him, including his money, but it had simply disappeared.

Ten years later, the shepherd was sitting by the fire reminiscing, feeling very sad and alone, particularly since his son had been killed in the war, when there was a knock on the door. It was his friend, the gamekeeper, who asked the shepherd if he had heard the latest: the old peddler's ghost had been seen 'stalking abroad'. The gamekeeper noticed that his friend looked very shaken, if not fearful, when he told him the news.

After the gamekeeper had said his farewells and left for the night, the shepherd started to tremble. He muttered away to himself as he went across to lift a floorboard near the fire and as he did so, he kept looking round to make sure that nobody was watching. From this hidden place he brought out a tin box, which was full of bank notes worth over £100. He poured half a bottle of whisky down his throat to steady his nerves, slipped the notes into his pocket and went out into the night.

The next morning a group of children were on their way to school when they saw something strange, a large, lumpen bundle, at the foot of an old birch tree. Frightened, they rushed to school to tell their teacher, who immediately went back with other adults to investigate. It was the shepherd, rambling and delirious, covered in blood and looking as if he had been beaten, with bank notes scattered all around him. Before long everyone in the district had heard what had happened and realised that it was no ghost that the shepherd had seen. He had come across the rotten stump of a tree which had two decaying branches at either side and had taken it for the ghost of the peddler. As someone remarked at the time, 'this withered stump was the supernatural visitant'. The shepherd's imagination had got the better of him and he must have fought the tree thinking that it was the peddler's ghost seeking revenge. However, although retribution was made, the shepherd died a few days later, apparently from shock.

It has been said that brownies used to frequent the Highlands and two of the last to be written about were said to have been in service with the ancient family of Tullochgorum, in Strathspey. The male was known as Brownie Clod, a cheerful character who liked to play tricks on his fellow-servants and used to throw clods at passers-by, hence his name. The female, Maig Mhullaich, or 'Maag Vullach', would report other servants to the master and mistress of the house if work had not been carried out correctly. Often called Hairy Mag because of her superabundance of hair, she was both honest and hardworking. She was a quick and thorough housekeeper and apparently the table would be set in a flash, items floating through the air and nestling in their proper places while she remained invisible. A pity these brownies were not around today!

Another brownie was known to help at the Doune, a large house in Rothiemurchus, during the night. A bowl of cream would be left out every evening as payment for clearing up and washing the dishes so that in the morning, when the household wakened, everything would be clean and bright. One night, however, the brownie accidentally dropped all of the cutlery, which clattered onto the floor, wakening the family. The laird, bad-tempered because of being disturbed, went down to the kitchen and, before the brownie could put on his shoes, chased him out of the house. Knowing that he could not get back into fairyland without his shoes, the brownie sat down by a tree and sobbed uncontrollably until, eventually, a shoemaker stopped and asked what the matter was. On hearing the sad tale, the shoemaker said that he had come from Lynwilg to make dancing shoes for the laird's daughters, but had a few scraps of leather left in his bag and would quickly make little shoes for him. The brownie was delighted and immediately gathered special herbs to make a green dye which he rubbed on his new shoes, thus giving them the fairy powers required to get back to his own land. What was left of the mixture he gave to the shoemaker as a reward for his kindness, telling him to put it on the dancing shoes. He said that the shoes would not turn green but, instead, would last for ever. The brownie returned to fairyland and the shoemaker delivered three pairs of dancing shoes to the laird for his three daughters, who then became amazing dancers. When the old shoemaker died, we are told that his secret died with him. I can only presume that this story must have come from fairyland!

In the past, books about fairies, witches and other ethereal beings tended to be written in a factual manner, as though such spirits really existed. There is no hint of scepticism in the way the stories were told and they were passed on by credible people. Through time, however, story-tellers have moulded tales to fit their beliefs, not always in accordance with ancient Highland Celtic tradition, in which such creatures were felt to be generally, though clearly not always, benign towards humans, and often guided them through difficulties or saved their lives.

Kaledon Naddair, a writer whose works include several on the subject of Otherworld beings, notes that our ancestors, 'living in an unspoilt natural world, unhampered by inappropriate Christianised conditioning, had far more finely tuned physical senses and more opened psychic awareness; thus it should come as no surprise to read that they more often perceived these Otherworld beings, and with much greater clarity'. He also speculates that the modern reluctance to believe in them could stem from 'the fear of the unknown, and fear of the primeval and "wild" in a comfortably civilizied world'. Would people freely admit to supporting this theory or would they rather wrap themselves in the cosy cocoon of explained science, I wonder?

18

Hidden Loch

I first walked across the estate known as Ben Alder, which surrounds and includes the mountain of that name, one summer in the late 1960s when Euan and I were staying at Halfway House. Though the midges were at their worst, we set off for a whole day with our labrador, taking a picnic with us. The soft, gentle colours of the Highland scenery were as beautiful as ever, particularly the hills beyond Loch Ericht. The few dwellings we saw were typical of all the estates in those parts.

Recently I went back there, having arranged to meet the head stalker, Ian Crichton, at his house on the estate, which meant a nine-mile journey along the side of Loch Ericht. As directed, I took a little road from Dalwhinnie, making my way to a track under a railway bridge, beyond which I was faced with a security barrier and duly punched in a secret code-number on its keypad. I thought it most incongruous to find such a system miles away from anywhere, in a wild place that was otherwise unchanged since I was last there, thirty years before. Habits have had to change, however, for it is now necessary to protect not only private property but also privacy. As instructed, I turned to the right, driving between two pillars, the first of many, and was now travelling parallel to the wall at the south edge of the loch. The wall was neat and level, a hard line against the gentle hills behind,

Drumochter to the left and Ardverikie to the right. Gradually, the mist came down between those two hills and hid the mountains at the end of the eighteen-mile loch. It was a dismal day, but the mist suddenly lifted to reveal the most breathtaking views.

As I motored along the side of the loch, I watched little white horses breaking the surface of the water. The serenity of the atmosphere took me back into the past, when, instead of cars, there would have been only clansmen, horses and wild animals by this loch, and I felt out of place. Had I seen apparitions of those long dead round the next corner, I would not have been surprised. Fir trees on the loch-side frequently obliterated glimpses of the water and the hills beyond, and branches overhead blocked the sky, but once out in the open, however low the clouds, the landscape was glorious. Across a pillared bridge lay an impressive group of buildings, the factor's house and offices, which were linked by an arch. It looked like a film set and I felt privileged to be allowed into this hidden, secret place. There was another security gate to negotiate, so I put in the next code and the gates majestically opened, after which I drove another five and a half miles, passing yet another magnificent stone building with many towers and turrets. Eventually I came to the main gates of Ben Alder Lodge, which I knew I had to pass to reach the head stalker's house. I was suddenly jerked back into the real world by two friendly dogs greeting me in the carpark of a new-looking house set in grounds which extended to the loch and hills beyond.

Ian and Christine Crichton had lived in that lovely place with their family for eighteen years and before that, Ian had been employed by the Deer Commission. He had long experience of working with red and roe deer; he was of the 'old school' and believed that good stalking should not be easy. If it was not hard work, then it was not worth doing. He believed that it should always be done entirely on foot; to him it was anathema for a hunter to be driven to within a few yards of an easy shot. 'I never

really think, "Oh, I'd better go to work!"' Ian said. He clearly loved
his job, finding it a joy to go out every morning, never knowing
what kind of day it would be, for each was so different. Often he
would see a beast amongst a herd on the hillside and know
instinctively that this was the one he would get, even when the
circumstances made success unlikely. He was usually absolutely
right. In a remote place and living so close to nature, I could easily
imagine such an instinct developing, particularly in a man with
many years of experience.

Ponies were bred and broken-in on the estate for the purpose of
riding or stalking. Preferring the traditional way of bringing deer
down from the hill, Ian would use ponies whenever possible, but
if it were not feasible to do this, the stag or hind would be dragged
down to the loch, slipped off the rocks into a boat and then ferried
across to the other side. Throughout Ben Alder estate there are
pony paths, many of which are 100 years old; all are continually
upgraded and new ones are made. Ian told me that three boys are
hired for six months every year to maintain them according to his
exact specification. To deter motorcycles, the paths are deliberately
kept narrow, suitable only for ponies or passing hillwalkers.

Some have drowned in the loch. Ian recalled a January day
when, having brought a beast down to the edge of the loch and
pulled it onto a flat rock, he stepped into the boat and gave the
rope a jerk, hoping to pull the deer in beside him. Needless to
say, this sudden movement got the hind into the vessel, but sent
Ian shooting off the other side into the water. If it was freezing
cold at the edge, he said, it would have been absolutely perishing
in the centre of the loch. Indeed, a few years previously a boat
had capsized way out, throwing a party of fishermen into the icy
water. One of the gentlemen died from hypothermia before he
reached the hospital in Fort William, whilst being transported
there by helicopter.

As I looked out over the loch, the sun had just lifted the mist
and all seemed magical, as if nothing awful could ever happen

there. The water was clear, as blue as the skies had become, and the heather-clad hills stood in sharp contrast behind. This was the part of the world I had once known so well and all of a sudden yearned to go back to. The calling of the hills never leaves you, it seems.

Though most people are wary of the potential dangers of Highland lochs, some are also drawn to them in times of trouble or need. About thirty years ago, the young wife of a ghillie who worked at Ben Alder died and, in his grief, her husband threw her wedding-ring into a little loch close to Loch Ericht, where it doubtless remains, as perhaps do his thoughts and memories of her. The ring has never been found, but recently, when the water level dropped considerably, Ian observed old piers and other objects exposed in the shallow waters. Among these was an old iron mallet – perhaps it belonged to a former employee on the estate, who, fed up with his workload, flung the tool into the water!

Geordie Oswald, who was the last head stalker at Ben Alder, used to assure Ian that his position was an important one; he was of the opinion that head stalkers were to be held in high esteem and treated with respect. When the visitors came for stalking, Geordie used to say, 'They think they bloody own the place, but I bloody own it; they are only here for a few weeks!' The previous owner of the estate had respected and trusted his head stalker implicitly, for he was well aware that his skills were to be prized. Following a stalk, if the laird returned feeling more than a little displeased with himself, he would pass by the head stalker's cottage, his mood quite remorseful and humbled, knowing that his fine stalker was far more accomplished in the art than he.

There came a time when Geordie began to have problems with his knees and was obliged to retire to his cottage. Often he would be sitting in front of the open fire in his living room when suddenly a hat would be thrown into the middle of the floor and the voice of the laird would be heard to say, 'I am sorry, Geordie,

I am sorry!' It was because he had let his head stalker down, either by shooting the wrong beast or leading a poor stalk! It appeared that Geordie was indeed the boss there as far as hunting was concerned.

Stalking is a fairly safe sport, as long as the hunter has respect for the rifle. Stalkers take out guests hoping that they are proficient and safe in their practice, and they expect those they lead to follow instructions. The only time a gun can be unsafe is when it is treated with disregard or used to destructive ends. By way of illustration, Ian told me that about ten years previously the body of a young man had been found by two hillwalkers at the top of one of the shoulders of Ben Alder, overlooking the Loch of the Pass (Loch a Beahlach). He had committed suicide by shooting himself in the heart with a replica Remington .44, and was found sitting upright, wedged behind a rock. A cranio-facial reconstruction of his face was shown on *Crimewatch* and he was identified as a Frenchman who had been missing for many months. After his parents were alerted, a helicopter was organised to take them to the top of Ben Alder. Their son had found peace in the vast spaces of the mountains. By coincidence, on the very day that the body was discovered, Ian's son had climbed Ben Alder, his first Munro, accompanied by his father.

At the south-west end of the loch stands a famous bothy, known locally both as McCook's Cottage and Ben Alder Cottage, the latter being its original name, which is still used on maps and in hillwalkers' guidebooks. One of the stories about it records the heroism of the local doctor, who ventured out to it in the middle of winter when McCook was extremely ill with pneumonia. His daughter had been dispatched to send a telegram asking for urgent medical assistance, which meant walking about eight miles over the hills to Rannoch Post Office, only to find nothing could be done for her there. She was obliged to walk several miles more to try again at Bridge of Gaur, where she had better luck, for a telegram was sent on her behalf to Kingussie Post Office. The message was subsequently transmitted to Laggan, having virtually gone round the area in full circle. The doctor, who lived on the outskirts of Laggan, was alerted, cranked up his old Ford motorcar forthwith and made his way to Dalwhinnie, accompanied by two fit men, who had brought with them long ropes as a precaution. By this time the snow was falling fast, so the doctor was dubious whether he and his party would be able to get any further than Drumochter, let alone up the track to Ben Alder Cottage, along Loch Ericht. Inevitably the car had to be abandoned at Dalwhinnie because the snow had begun to drift and was by then far too deep to continue. The rest of the journey had to be made on foot.

Because of the appalling weather and rapidly melting snow, the mountain streams had become roaring torrents which cascaded down the hillsides. The doctor and his two companions had to use their ropes to climb up the sides of these waterfalls until it was possible to cross them, after which they had to make a descent on the other side. Considering there were about twenty streams, this journey took time and it must have seemed like twenty miles instead of the twelve miles that they had to travel. Safely reaching the patient, the doctor examined him, administered emergency medication, then promptly fell on the floor, unconscious.

The other two men looked after the doctor, making him comfortable and giving him sustenance until he was able to make his return journey. Once he had sufficiently recovered, he walked back to retrieve his car and then drove straight home. McCook received regular parcels of medicine by post and made a full recovery, thanks to the doctor, who later received the Carnegie medal for his dedication.

The land surrounding Ben Alder, like other parts of the Highlands, was subject to cattle-rustling in the past and there is a stirring tale of two young housewives who, alone together in the sheilings (pastures), managed to outwit a gang of thieves.

Their cattle had been disturbed and had started to bellow, so the girls, in the absence of their menfolk, decided to deal with the situation themselves; they guessed that it was probably men from Lochaber who had come to steal their animals. Gathering up all the pieces of metal that they could find and tying them together, they rushed outside to face the enemy. One girl had a deep voice like a man's and began to shout loudly whilst the other, in a high-pitched tone, made a call used to gather the cattle, both simultaneously shaking their bundles of metal. They made such a racket that the rustlers were convinced there was an ambush and fled back to Lochaber. The ruse succeeded and the herd was saved.

Ben Alder also has a famous historical connection, for within its bounds can be found Prince Charlie's Cave, known as 'The Cage', which was one of Cluny Macpherson's hiding-places during the uprisings of 1745. Near the end of his difficult years of seclusion, Cluny entertained the prince in this cave before he made his escape to France, where he died the following year. Whatever his tribulations, Cluny could not have wished for more beautiful scenery. Although there may have been few changes in the contours of the hills since then, the way of life, inevitably, is quite different nowadays.

I left Ben Alder estate that afternoon exactly as I had found it earlier, a mysterious, serene place such as one might find in a fairytale, where time seemed to stand still. One cannot blame the new owners for keeping their jewel under lock and key, for it is surely a treasure far too precious to be disturbed.

19

The Shelter

DR Isabel Frances Grant, a descendant of one of the senior branches of Clan Grant, the Grants of Tullochgorm, was born in 1887. Her Mackintosh mother's family home was in Strathdearn, but because of her father's military service abroad, she spent much time as a child with her paternal grandparents in London. Her grandfather, Field Marshal Sir Patrick Grant, had briefly been commander-in-chief in India in 1857 and subsequently governor of Malta, governor of the Chelsea Royal Hospital for old or disabled soldiers and Gold-Stick-in-Waiting to Queen Victoria. Though Dr Grant was taught solely by a governess, attending neither school nor university, her inquiring mind and passion for tradition led her to gather information throughout her life, thus continually furthering her education of her own accord.

She started to write in the 1920s under the name I.F. Grant, avoiding the use of her Christian names to disguise the fact that she was 'a mere woman', as she put it, from her readers. The best-known of her twenty or more books is *Highland Folkways*, which depicts the life and culture of the people. Reprinted many times, it is now considered an international classic and is widely used in schools and universities as part of the curriculum.

During her long lifetime she was reputed to be one of the greatest Highland historians and was, moreover, the pioneer of the Folk Museum movement in Scotland. Between the two

World Wars she worked as a researcher at the London School of
Economics and in 1930 became the organising secretary of the
Highland Exhibition. As a result of her great interest in such
work, she collected a huge amount of traditional Highland
material, including items that were used in daily life, not only the
more obvious domestic and farming implements but also small
items that were usually taken for granted, such as wooden
latches. Not surprisingly, her efforts were greatly appreciated by
the National Museum of Antiquities, its staff and resources to
undertake such work being in perennial short supply.

In 1935, a combination of her own money and a legacy from
an aunt enabled Dr Grant to open a museum for her collection
in the United Free Church at Martyrs Bay on Iona. It was the
very first folk museum in the United Kingdom and was named
Am Fasgadh, which is Gaelic for 'the shelter'. However, she later
decided to move the entire contents of this establishment back
to the mainland, where she opened a second Am Fasgadh in the
old Free Church on the Glentruim side of Laggan Bridge. The
move proved difficult because Iona lacked a pier, which meant
that all her packing-cases had to be loaded onto a small tender
and rowed out to a larger vessel for the crossing.

No sooner had she arrived at Laggan to open her new museum
than the Second World War broke out and she was called up for
training purposes. Luckily, thanks to her exalted connections in
army circles (her paternal great-grandfather was Lord Gough, a
hero of Britain's imperial wars during the first half of the
nineteenth century), it was recommended that she should be
relieved of her duties. Nevertheless, she had to travel south
occasionally because of her involvement in the Economic Warfare
Group, a branch of the Secret Service. During these short periods
Am Fasgadh was closed. It was said that her mission was to assist
with the task of upsetting German efforts by flooding the
Fatherland with counterfeit money. Meanwhile, Am Fasgadh was
doing so well that she decided to move her exhibition to

Kingussie in 1944, when she succeeded in purchasing Old Pitmain Lodge, once the home of the duke of Gordon's factor in Badenoch.

Dr Grant had been impressed by the open-air museums she had visited in Scandinavia. She felt it was regrettable that Scotland lacked such imaginative means to illuminate its past and was inspired to open something of her own along similar lines. Pitmain Lodge was renovated to house her original collection and stone-by-stone reconstructions of typical black-houses from the Western Highlands and Isles were built in the grounds. Thus was created Britain's first open-air folk museum. The Scottish universities supported the enterprise from her retiral in 1954 until the mid 1970s, after which the Highland Regional Council took over and has been running it successfully ever since.

George Dixon knew Dr Grant well, frequently visiting her during her long Edinburgh retirement. He found it fascinating to listen to her sweeping overviews of the last centuries. She once complimented him by stating that his 'knowledge of Strathspey was encyclopaedic'. George, ever intrigued by the history of the Highlands, had started to jot down interesting tales and anecdotes at an early age in his own homemade notepads. He first met Dr Grant in the 1940s during the October potato holidays when he was about twelve and had travelled by bus all the way from Grantown-on-Spey to visit the Folk Museum in Kingussie. George said that he was a 'timid cratur' as he knocked on the door of Am Fasgadh, which was opened by a tall, gracious lady, who happened to be Dr Grant herself. She told him that the museum was closed for the season, but noticing his bitter disappointment, particularly when she learnt how far he had come, she took pity on him and invited him in. He was shown round the whole museum. His day was unforgettable.

George told me that Dr Grant's memory for people and events in the nineteenth century was quite phenomenal. Apart from her paternal grandfather, she also well remembered her maternal grandfather, who had been the principal male mourner at the funeral of Sir Aeneas Mackintosh, who had become the clan chief in 1870. As a young girl, she had attended a function in 1894 at Castle Grant, Grantown, in honour of her grandfather, Field-Marshal Sir Patrick Grant, a respected native of Strathspey and famed as a fierce warrior in his day, on the occasion of his ninetieth birthday. She remembered looking out of one of the castle windows and seeing a long line of Strathspey people walking up the drive to attend the celebrations. An older relative had also told her that, as was court practice, her grandfather had always been obliged to stand in the presence of Her Majesty, but that in his eighties, when age made him a bit unsteady on his pins, he was told to sit! In 1976, eighty-two years later and by then very lame, or 'hirply' as she called it, Dr Grant gave her last public lecture, in her capacity as honorary president of the Grantown Society. 'All present stood in tribute to her,' reported George, 'as she slowly inched her way up to the speaker's table.' She made an unforgettable speech which was both entertaining and warm-hearted.

During the time she lived at Heriot Row in the 1970s she fell over twice, breaking a leg on each occasion. Because her injuries made it increasingly difficult for her to manage alone, she decided to move into a home for the elderly in Lennox Row, where she would be looked after. Several years later she unfortunately developed cancer and had to go into hospital for a major operation. Though she made a good recovery from the surgery, she died of a heart attack at the age of nearly 100 the following week. Right up to the end of her days she continued to write books, even when her eyesight began to fail and she had to resort to recording her work. Dr Grant was indeed a courageous lady, with formidable intelligence, who encouraged children and adults alike to treasure their past. She will always be remembered for her wealth of knowledge, which, thanks to her delightful books, continues to reach every generation.

Today the museum contains a vast collection of items, many of which are of national and international value, most originally gathered together by Dr Grant, although there have been later additions. In 1976 the Museum Services, under the aegis of the Highland Region Advisory Services, appointed Ross Noble as the Highland Curator, a post he held for twenty-seven years.

Ross and I both remember when the River Gynack broke its banks in 1975; water gushed into Am Fasgadh, through a door on one side and out of another at the back. The cellars, where valuable curling stones were stored, were completely flooded, as were the black-houses, all sustaining substantial damage. The water had to be pumped out and sand-bags were placed everywhere. Meanwhile, salmon swam freely, in their newfound river, along Spey Street in Kingussie! Such flooding must have been a frequent occurrence in the past, for an old article in a magazine stated that once, when Spey Street was inundated, parishioners were forced to take a boat to church for communion. The boatman, unprincipled and greedy, gave no notice of suddenly raising his prices, demanding sixpence for the fare: 'No sixpence, no crossing' was his view. Several people could not afford such an exorbitant sum, and, thus, missed the Sunday service. An old lady in her nineties was among those turned back, even although she promised to pay at a later date. I once read in a newspaper from 1850 a description of the Sabbath as 'the greatest friend of physical health and mental refreshment'. How sad to deprive an old lady of that comfort!

Ross continued essential pioneering work on behalf of Am Fasgadh and in the 1980s secured 85 acres of land on the outskirts of Newtonmore for the next phase of the development of the museum. Several old buildings were purchased, then dismantled and rebuilt on the new museum site. One such was MacPherson's tailor's shop, a former gentlemen's tailors and outfitters which had eventually become a garden shed on the golf course road in Newtonmore. It was dismantled, taken to its new position and rebuilt. The Shell garage was brought from Kingussie and now houses the museum's collection of buses; the Leanach church came from Culloden Moor, where it had long sat at the edge of the battlefield; and Knockbain school was actually built in the 1920s but has been recreated as a 1930s school. Ardverikie Estate provided a functional sawmill and the post office came from Glenlivet. More buildings have been added over the years, although Altlarie, the working farm, was already in situ, which was one of the reasons the museum was eager to purchase the land. Its various buildings were bought from the landowner and the crofting rights from Bob Kirk, who used to be the Home Farm manager at Glentruim. The nineteenth-century farm house was completely restored, which meant that all additions and items not belonging to that era were removed and made good.

This new open-air museum, built to complement Am Fasgadh and named the Highland Folk Museum, is situated in a prime location off the old A9 between Newtonmore and Kingussie. It celebrated its first full year in 1996. The site is divided into four areas: Altlarie, the museum's working farm; the open-air museum, the aim of which is the creation of a typical Highland community by means of relocated buildings; and The Pinewoods and Baile Gean, the museum's unique reconstruction of an early eighteenth-century Highland township.

Other additions include a railway halt, shops and dwellings such as a tin cottage, many of which have furnishings of their particular era. The working farm is stocked with indigenous animals that can be seen wandering at large. The whole experience takes each visitor back in time, for the guides are all dressed for the part they play, wearing clothes of days gone by. On the subject of visitors' comments, Ross Noble told me that many said they had not really known what they were coming to, could not relate to the culture and were truly perplexed by some of the history. For instance, some were worried that there had been no sanitation 200 years ago. One person reported the museum for mistreating its pigs because of the muddy state of their field, unaware that Tamworth pigs love digging up stones and moving them around. The inspectors who came as a result of the complaint were amused. Many visitors from urban backgrounds were so removed from any sort of natural landscape that they had never seen horses being shod. For them, to watch hot metal being nailed onto the horses' hooves and smell burning could be disturbing and the process had to be carefully explained. Children were excited to watch the cows being milked, some truly not knowing where milk came from. This magnificent living museum is a most imaginative way in which to educate children about the former life and traditions of the Highlands. School parties come from all over the world to visit it and it provides a pleasant day out for all age groups. Little wonder this enterprise was presented with the 'Scottish Museum of the Year' award by Princess Anne in 2000, a major accolade. The following year, it received the Heritage Education Award and in 2002 it was nominated for the European Museum Award. What a tribute to Dr I.F. Grant, the founder of Am Fasgadh, who encouraged us to discard nothing of traditional value!

★★★

One of my best friends, Margaret Bennett, lived in Kingussie when our children were young. She eventually left the area to work in the School of Scottish Studies in Edinburgh, but having a great love of Kingussie, took every opportunity to return. Before her students sat their degree exams, she would take them on a field trip to Am Fasgadh, which she felt was the perfect teaching environment to let them experience first-hand what they had learned from lectures and books. She used to say that you can read all you like about a thatched house, but until you saw it, touched it, lowered your head as you walked through the door into the dim light, then sat by the peat fire in the middle of the

189

floor, you would never really be acquainted with the former Highlander's home. During these visits, the students would stay at the local youth hostel for the weekend and everyone had an active part to play. They would find themselves making brose for breakfast, gathering nettles to make soup, looking at the flora in the area, watching a shinty match, or generally appreciating whatever other experience Margaret could weave into the time available.

Ross Noble was very pleased to have such a link with the university and the members of staff in the black-house generally knew what to expect. The group of students would come in just as though they were visitors to the household, smell the peat and taste the oatcakes or scones that were being made, and before long a ceilidh would materialise. The archaic atmosphere was further conjured up and enhanced by the fact that many of those who worked at the museum wore clothes from the past, and indeed Margaret herself has always been known for her long, traditional skirts. She would soon be sitting by the fire telling stories, singing songs and generally recreating the way people lived in former times. Tourists who happened to pass by would have no idea that this extra dimension was not a daily occurrence, but a privilege they had happened to stumble upon: a session with one of Scotland's foremost folklorists. Her voice is known worldwide, for she is also one of Scotland's finest Gaelic singers. But, as one critic once put it, 'Dr Bennett wears her scholarship very lightly'. In fact she never mentions it and being entirely at ease with the traditions she seeks to perpetuate, has a way of encouraging her audiences to join in. I am sure that her students will always remember those happy days.

Martyn, Margaret's son, grew up with our children and often came to Glentruim for the day. When the snow lay thick, Margaret and I would watch our youngsters sledge down the banks on tin trays that I had been given as a child. One of the trays had transfers of Alice in Wonderland printed on it when it was new, but long years of sledging had worn all the pictures away. Sometimes Martyn used to play the bagpipes for us, much to the delight of ourselves and our guests, for he was very young and the pipes were the same size as he was. At one stage he used to have to turn the instrument upside-down to tune the drones, for his arms were not long enough to reach them; Margaret and I had difficulty in keeping a straight face as we watched this little person trying to figure out how to achieve this. As anyone who ever heard him play would know and anyone who listened to his music could hear, he was an outstanding musician, even as a child. When he and Margaret moved to Edinburgh, Martyn played the bagpipes for his audition at the City of Edinburgh Music School, becoming the first child in Scotland to be accepted on the 'noble instrument', thus paving the way for the recognition of Scotland's music and instruments. Martyn, who was always grateful to his teacher in Kingussie for giving him the best possible grounding in music, later became proficient in several other instruments. As a student at the Royal Scottish Academy of Music and Drama he became an outstanding classical violinist and composer. Sadly, Martyn died at the beginning of 2005, a huge loss to the musical world. His exquisite orchestral composition, 'MacKay's Memoirs', was commissioned and performed for the opening of the Scottish Parliament in 1999. The CD of the piece is fittingly dedicated to Martyn, 'a passionate and innovative genius, a generous warm soul, and a true friend'.

20

Games and Gatherings

WHEN I think of shinty, in my mind's eye I see Robert Ritchie (Rob), the 'the King of Shinty', as he is sometimes called. Rob was born in the 1940s at Croftdhu, his grandmother's house, which was situated on a hill above the Skye of Curr Heather Centre, near Dulnain Bridge. His mother, alone at the time because her husband was serving in the Second World War, had decided to stay there for his birth. That house has since gone and today only its shell remains, but Rob remembers it well from his childhood. When he spoke of his granny, he told me that she was said to have second sight, and was also able to cure sick animals, which were brought to her by the local folk; she had a great knowledge of herbs and plants and their diverse healing properties.

The dreaded news, familiar to so many at that time, came in the form of a telegram informing Rob's grandmother that his uncle, Donald Ritchie, who had been serving in the Seaforth Highlanders, was 'missing, presumed dead'. Weeks went past with no word, but his grandmother had great faith and remained optimistic. One day, she had just walked round the corner of her cottage when a big, black dog appeared beside her. It was only there for a few seconds before completely vanishing. This, she felt, was a sign; it confirmed to her that her son was alive. Indeed, she was correct, for it was later discovered that Donald had been

193

taken prisoner and was being held in a Polish camp. After the war was over, Rob's grandmother was informed that Donald had been allowed to hide in the home of a Polish family. These people had been captured at the same time as himself, and during the trying days of internment, he would speak to the daughter of the family through the fence that separated the male and female camps. He was full of admiration for her courage: she had put her own life at risk by harbouring a fugitive in her home and had forfeited her freedom and all of her possessions, including her rings, which had been ripped off her fingers. The young couple fell in love 'through the wires' and ultimately escaped together, ending their days as a married couple in Boat of Garten, near Aviemore. Rob's father also returned safely to his family home in Newtonmore after D-Day.

When Rob was young, there were shinty enthusiasts in all of the schools in the district, including Newtonmore, and they started the game early in their lives. These boys took every opportunity they could to play, the highlight of each week being Saturday, when they supported their players at matches against visiting teams on the Eilan, which is the shinty field in Newtonmore.

At that time, the headmaster of Newtonmore Primary School was Donald Finlayson, a native of Braes in Skye, who encouraged his pupils to acquire skills in the game. Rob told me how proud he was the first time they won the Mackay Cup in the Scottish Primary Schools Championship and how he later found himself amongst those who were subsequently deemed the very backbone of the future, highly successful, Newtonmore team. Long jump, high jump and running were other activities that the school fostered and because of the schoolmaster's enthusiasm, Rob and others won Inter-Primary School Cups for the whole of Badenoch and Strathspey, which was commendable for such a small primary school. This was just the beginning for Rob: when he went to the high school in Kingussie, he achieved a medal in the John Macpherson Cup, a secondary school championship, and became a senior sports champion whilst himself still a junior. His abilities went from strength to strength and he soon found himself representing Newtonmore in competitions all over the country.

When they all left school at fifteen, many of the other boys found employment as joiners or bricklayers, but no such job was available to Rob, so he took work on the hills, assisting with grouse shooting and stalking on various estates in the district. He was used to this, having spent time beating during the summer holidays from the age of nine, as did many of his peers. Another favourite career for boys between the ages of fourteen and seventeen was the army cadet force of the Cameron Highlanders. They learnt how to march and drill, and attended annual camps, which had indoor and outdoor shooting ranges for firing-practice. Above all, however, they were taught discipline. Rob excelled during his time in the cadets, once achieving five medals for running and jumping, which were presented by the famous Major General Wimberly, Company Officer of the 51st Highland Division at Alamein. He would have made a good soldier, but chose the police force instead, enjoying every exciting minute of the seven years he served in Glasgow. He played shinty for them and was also a member of their tug-of-war team when they won a Scottish Championship. However, a time came when Rob longed to return home, back to the true land of shinty and Highland games.

In the old days, it would have been difficult to find any young boy in Badenoch and Strathspey who did not play shinty; today there are unfortunately other more modern distractions to keep many away from the playing-fields. The young used to grow up with the game and they progressed with their teams from primary school years to manhood, a fervent team spirit uniting them in their ambition to win.

Shinty, Scotland's national sport, is an ancient game traditionally known in Gaelic as camanachd. It was brought to Scotland by Irish invaders some 1,400 years ago, and is derived from the Irish game of hurling; it is still played throughout the Highlands and elsewhere. Though it resembles hockey in some respects, it has twelve, not eleven, in a team, taller goalposts, and is played with a small, hard, wooden ball and broadly hooked sticks. The object of the game is for each team to send the ball beyond the boundary on either side and the skill is to strike the ball the furthest distance towards the opponents' boundary. It is said that shinty keeps both body and mind alert, and it is one of the best sports for building muscles and promoting agility, but some general rules may also indicate how rough and dangerous the game was in the past: 'The caman [club/stick] is to be used for no other purpose than that of propelling the ball; neither to trip the foot of an opponent nor in any way to molest him, except to turn away his club that you may gain the ball.' Pushing and shouldering is also forbidden. However, when you watch an aggressive game played by forceful and often overpowering men, it is hard to know whether there are any rules at all; the game obviously requires speed, strength and endurance in particular.

The Camanachd Association, the ruling body of the game, was formed well over a century ago. Certain traditions are associated with the sport: at halftime, players used to drink port with lemon and oranges; at the corners of the field there would have been pails of water containing oatmeal, and players would drink the cloudy water, which was considered very fortifying. Others would bring handfuls of oatmeal for the same purpose, to be kept in their pockets until required. A couple of raw eggs might also be swallowed whole to provide energy before a match. Well into the twentieth century there were great celebrations at New Year, when whole estates would gather at the Eilan for a fifty-a-side contest, and the Cluny Macpherson of that time would supply hot drinks and oatcakes. At Christmas, too, there would be great festivities on the shinty field and parishes would play against each other.

Superstition would sometimes get in the way of rational thinking, for if members of a shinty team were on the way to a match and passed a white horse in a field, it was considered bad luck. They might therefore have to take a long detour, if possible, in order to reach their destination without passing the animal. Taking photographs of the team before leaving for a match was thought to bring even worse luck. In one particular story from the early 1900s, a green shawl was the source of a superstition. When the Kingussie shinty team, then considered the champions, were travelling by bus to play a match in Laggan, they noticed a green shawl hanging from one of the branches of a rowan tree at the side of the road. Unknown to them, the old lady who owned the shawl had wished them bad luck as they passed by, which unfortunately influenced the result, for they lost the match later that day. Having heard this story, when the Laggan team planned to play against Lord Lovat's team, they became extremely anxious, dreading to pass under this rowan tree. They need not have worried, for as they went by the old lady wished them good luck, even promising them success. The game had not been going well for the Laggan team and it looked as if they were going to lose, but in the last half hour of the game they picked up their score and won, just as the old lady had predicted. A few weeks later, the same team was to play against Kyles of Bute at the Kingussie fields. They duly set off, this time with no misgivings regarding the green shawl, for they had recently achieved a succession of victories and were feeling very confident. When they passed the rowan tree, some members of the team had hoped to see the green shawl or even the old lady, thus ensuring their luck, but it was not to be: there was nothing there, which they took as a bad omen. The ensuing game ended in defeat, much to the disappointment of the team.

It was said that when Kingussie played Newtonmore on its home ground, they seldom lost a game, whereas it was also believed that Newtonmore 'held the key for the Eilan' and that they were invincible there. It became apparent much later, however, that every time Kingussie's team visited the Eilan for a match, an old lady was seen shaking a green shawl in front of their coach. After a succession of wins for Newtonmore, the two teams were playing once again on the Eilan, but this time no magic shawl was observed and strangely enough, the championship cup was taken home to Kingussie. Could this have been anything to do with the absence of the green shawl? Those from Newtonmore had their suspicions.

***

People travel from all over the country to participate in or watch Highland games, which offer a varied selection of events. Over the years Rob entered many of the competitions, such as hammer throwing, ball and chain throwing, and shot-putting. Although he won championships across the world for tossing the caber, he never became a professional because of his involvement in shinty, which took up most of his time. Shinty used to be a winter sport, for in the past most of the players worked during the summer, but now this has changed and it is played all year round.

Highland games, primarily a Scottish event, can be traced back over 1000 years, to the days when the ancient kings of Scotland and clan chiefs selected their strongest men and fastest runners as their bodyguards. It was not until 1848, however, the year Queen Victoria first attended a Braemar Highland Gathering, that Highland games drew the attention of the world. Today, they usually take place between May and September, very often held on the same weekend of each year in the same towns or villages, and attract thousands of people from both home and abroad. Because most of the Saturdays have now been pre-booked for so many years, some of the newly established Games have to be held on a Sunday, which would not have been welcomed in the past. These events are still attended by clan chiefs and local lairds, and in addition politicians, businessmen and others from all walks of life are amongst the spectators. These days a Chieftain of the Games is appointed, for a specific number of years, to preside over the day's events, assisted by a number of committee members. It is an exciting occasion, with a programme that generally includes pipe bands, solo pipers, Highland dancers, hill and track runners, as well as less traditional events. Meanwhile, in the centre of the arena, there might be a tug-of-war going on, or a dozen men in kilts pulling stones and metal balls, throwing hammers and weights, in height and distance competitions. One of the main attractions is tossing the caber, and as Rob so rightly said, 'When people attend these events, particularly when watching men throw 20-foot tree trunks about, they know that they are witnessing a unique Scottish happening.'

It is interesting to note that some of the events originate from games that were played long ago in times of leisure. Cannonballs were sometimes used for shot-putting in time of war and at the front doors of large houses there would often be hefty round stones, which visitors would pick up to prove their strength. I remember granite stones such as these at either side of Glentruim's front door, but they always remained firmly on the doorstep! Hammer-throwing is said to originate from a game played while customers waited for their horses to be shod at the blacksmith's anvil. Men would throw the blacksmith's hammers to see whose could reach the furthest point. Throwing the hammer is not always the safest of sports at Highland Games, for one or two of them have been known to land on dancing platforms, loudspeakers and tents, narrowly missing the crowds. A hammer once hurtled towards a pram, only to descend between the baby's legs as he slept, but though he was woken very abruptly, he was miraculously not hurt. On another occasion, a hill runner was struck by a bouncing hammer, but despite his injury he still managed to come in second. Throwing weights originated from a time when, for sport, workers would try to fling 2-cwt sacks of corn which had been soaked to make them heavier, over the ratters of a barn, in order to prove who was the strongest.

199

During clan battles, if a river was in spate, it was traditional for the strongest man to toss a tree across the raging torrent to act as a bridge so that the men could walk over to the other side. Then in the day of 'floats', when trees were felled and drifted downriver to sawmills, it was always the stronger men who succeeded in getting the timber into the middle of a fast current, which led to competition between the foresters. This, of course, was the origin of the sport of tossing the caber, one of the most famous and colourful events of Highland games, for it takes not only strength but also skill to heave and up-end a thick tree-trunk. Contrary to popular misconception, the aim of the contest is not to throw the caber as far as possible, but rather to make it stand on its end and then turn over. Rob described it to me as 'running at a clock, 12 o'clock being a perfect throw'. If no competitor manages to achieve this, then about six inches is sawn off the end and everyone tries again.

Over the years, non-professional competitors have often been rewarded with gifts rather than money, and certain articles would be fashionable in any given year. Rob won five calculators at one Games alone. On another occasion, when travelling-bags were popular, he received his fair share, but while he was in the changing tent one day, a runner came in and threw his prize down, saying, 'That's my seventeenth bag this year!'

Rob has won many caber-tossing championships over the years, one of which was held in the USA, where he and another local lad were the first Scotsmen to be invited to an event commemorating the anniversary of the Battle of Culloden. The two Cameron brothers from Dalwhinnie were also great winners, travelling all over the world to championships, and their sons, a total of five between the two of them, latterly competed against their fathers and beat them! At Newtonmore Games in the early 1970s, Rob and the Camerons, all well-known 'heavies' (those who compete in heavy events), were the only three men able to lift the Balavil Stone, a giant boulder of 291 lbs which had been taken out of the River Markie at Laggan. Rob was made chieftain of Forres Highland games in 2003, but before that particular honour, he had already received another: a shot-put was named the 'Rab Ritchie Stane' after him. 'That's when you know you've made it!' he observed.

Newtonmore Highland Games incorporates our Macpherson Clan Gathering, and Macphersons attend from all over the world. The A9 is closed for a short time that day while the Macpherson men march into the Eilan behind the pipe band, a magnificent occasion, vibrant with the colours of Highland dress and the stirring sound of Scottish music. All the clansmen are dressed in kilts; the visiting Macphersons who do not have one, and wish to march, borrow from other members before the event. This also happens at the Games, for no one is allowed to take part unless wearing traditional dress. It is surprising where the extra kilt might appear from – perhaps only at the last minute, between throws, a Highlander might come to the rescue, peel off his kilt and pass it on to a fellow competitor!

The first time I watched Newtonmore Highland Games and attended the Clan Gathering with Euan was in 1971. Thereafter, we went to both events without fail each year, missing only a couple, until 2001. The following year I returned alone. The Games have become busier and more competitive than ever in recent years, yet all the Macphersons appear to remain more or less the same, apart from the changes that time inevitably brings to us all. By our presence at the Games, we stay faithful to the clan. The Eilan is a fine place to meet annually, with the awe-inspiring rock rising beyond it, quietly waiting for us to shout its name, as we always do when gathered in the field: our war cry of old, our affirmation new: 'Creag Dhubh!'

Epilogue

Between the Two Lights

THE clan motto of the Macphersons is 'Touch not the cat bot a glove' (do not touch a wildcat without wearing gloves), and Badenoch and Strathspey could not be a more appropriate place for the clan seat. Crests bearing a rampant cat can be seen on gates and front doors throughout the valley, and when I lived at Glentruim, wildcat festivals were organised to encourage tourists to visit those villages now bypassed by the new A9. Although today these elusive creatures are infrequently seen, they were still numerous when I lived in the area and could be found on the hills of Glentruim, and in the bottom fields by the river. Some were even so bold as to sun themselves in our walled garden during the summer months.

Between the two lights, when day gradually fades into night, wild animals are forever in the process of beginning or ending a new adventure, oblivious to the passage of time as we know it. Their lives, in which the hours cannot be defined, are relentlessly part of a continuum broken only by pauses to regain energy or recover from attack, always driven by the primitive instinct of survival. Euan used to declare that there is no such thing as 'time', but most of us perceive it as measured. In retrospect, my days in the Highlands now seem to me to have belonged to another age, full of resonances of an even more distant past, when I was surrounded by constant signs and reminders of our

203

ancestors and clan battles, of legend and even of the supernatural world.

I never knew the Gaelic expression *eadair da solus*, which means 'between the two lights', until recently, but have always been aware of this special time, particularly while living at Glentruim. To me, it connects not only night with day but also takes the past through the present and into the future. Indeed, one of these passages of time has swept me from the peaceful wilderness of the Highlands to the busy, densely populated city of Edinburgh. I once opened my door to view wild gardens, with fields and woods stretching out to touch the glorious mountains beyond. Today I step out onto pavements that border cobbled streets, with tall buildings either side blocking any hope of even a glimpse of the nearby coastline. A short distance up the hill at the top of the street, however, there are extensive private gardens for the benefit of key-holders from nearby dwellings and, if you venture a little further still, the sea can just be seen as you look back between the rows of houses.

It would be impossible to live amongst landscapes such as those of the north of Scotland for over a quarter of a century without yearning to return and indeed, the Highland way of life cannot be replaced. Those were days of contentment, regardless of any adversity that may have come to pass, and the warmth of the local people was, and still is, unsurpassed.

Now living in a city of such culture, wealthy in both the arts and architecture, is an exciting new beginning for me. Before, I was alone with my music when I played the clarsach so often in my home. Here in Edinburgh I play my harp with a group of friends and, having taken up the violin, joined the RTO (The Really Terrible Orchestra): this music-making is both exciting and exhilarating. I have also found a welcome in Edinburgh and here too there is warm friendship. There is also much to enjoy in a city, particularly Edinburgh, which is, after all, only a couple of hours away from Badenoch and Strathspey.

Time may mean our whole life-span so far, or merely the hours in each of our days. It could refer to places where we have lived and flourished, to good times, or those we wish to forget. Just as each new day takes away darkness, replacing it with clear sunlight, so my affections are inevitably bound to drift forever between the two lights of my time, wherever I am – here, elsewhere, or in my former homeland, amongst the people of the wildcat country.

References

Aberdeen Journal, 310/5/1773 & 19/07/1773

An Essay on Ways and Means for Inclosing, Fallowing, Planting, by a Lover of his Country

BBC News Scotland

Brigadier Mackintosh of Borlum, A.M. Mackintosh

Colour Terminology & Psychology in All the Keltic Languages, Kaledon Naddair

Croft and Ceilidh, Colin MacDonald

Every-day Life on an Old Highland Farm, I.F. Grant

Highland Folkways, I.F. Grant

A Highlander Looks Back, Angus Macpherson

In the Glens Where I Was Young, Meta Humphrey Scarlett

In the Shadow of Cairngorm: Chronicles of the United Parishes of Abernethy and Kincardine, 1900, Rev. Dr. William Forsyth

Keltic Folk & Faerie Tales: Their Hidden Meaning Explored, Kaledon Naddair

Laggan's Legacy, A personal history of a Highland community, by its people

Lectures on the Mountains; or, the Highlands and Highlanders of Strathspey and Badenoch As They Were and As They Are, Second Series, William Grant Stewart

Legends of the Cairngorms, Affleck Gray

Letters of Two Centuries, Fraser McKintosh

Life amongst the Scots, Janet Adam Smith

Loads and Roads in Scotland: Land transport over 6000 Years,
A. Stenton & G. Stell (eds)

Memoirs of a Highland Lady (vols 1 and 2), Elizabeth Grant of
Rothiemurchus

Memories of my Youth, George MacPherson 1982 (unpublished*)*

Northern Scotland, G.W.S Barrow

Romantic Badenoch, Johnstone & Son

Scotland, Myth, Legend and Folklore, Stuart McHardy

Scottish Folk and Fairy Tales, selected and edited by Sir George
Douglas

A Strange and Wild Place, Sandra Macpherson

Tales of Whisky and Smuggling, Stuart McHardy

The Badenoch Record, Kingussie 1927–1929

The History of the Province of Moray, Rev. Lachlan Shaw

The Times